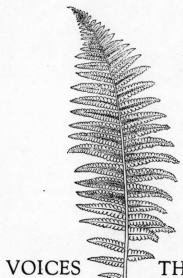

VOICES THAT ENDURED

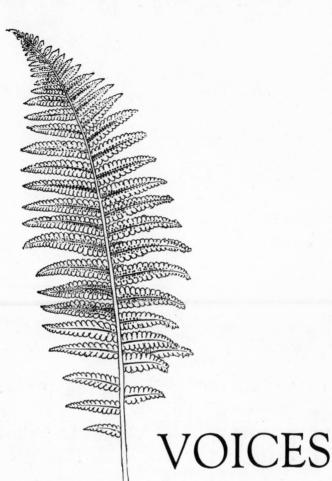

VOICES

STRINGFELLOW BARR

THAT ENDURED

THE GREAT BOOKS AND THE ACTIVE LIFE

PRENTICE-HALL, INC., ENGLEWOOD CLIFFS, N. J.

901.9
B268v

Voices That Endured: The Great Books and the Active Life
by Stringfellow Barr

Copyright © 1971 by Stringfellow Barr

ISBN 0–13–943738–X
Library of Congress Catalog Card Number: 70–138946

Printed in the United States of America • *T*

Prentice-Hall International, Inc., London
Prentice-Hall of Australia, Pty. Ltd., Sydney
Prentice-Hall of Canada, Ltd., Toronto
Prentice-Hall of India Private Ltd., New Delhi
Prentice-Hall of Japan, Inc., Tokyo

FOREWORD

This book was written in 1948 and was for one reason or another never published. Now that I have decided to publish it, I feel a certain regret that it should appear in the midst of so much betrayal of man's past, for it may easily be mistaken for an attempted answer to that horrendous academic question, what studies are "relevant"? Perhaps I shall be better understood if I report at the start for whom I did write this book: I wrote it for adults. In part I was moved by the remembered quality of those audiences to whom I sometimes lectured at the People's Institute at Cooper Union in New York in the early thirties. Those adult audiences always reminded me of George Bernard Shaw's remark about youth: that youth was such a wonderful thing it was a pity it had been wasted on the young. For although I have had exciting hours discussing these books with undergraduates, I have also had marvelous hours discussing them with adults. It was to discuss them once more, this time with adult readers, though not, alas, around a table as of yore, that I once set down what follows in this book.

Stringfellow Barr
February, 1971

CONTENTS

⚘

VOICES THAT ENDURED

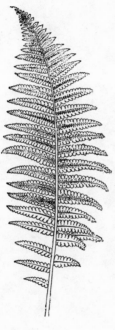

GREAT BOOKS AND THE ACTIVE LIFE

GREAT BOOKS AND THE ACTIVE LIFE

Thirty-three years ago a group of academics, of whom I made one, decided to abolish in one small college the specialized departments of the modern American elective system and the concern with disseminating up-to-date information and to replace these features with a common study of some hundred really great works of the Western tradition.

Here is the list as first published by this college, St. John's College in Annapolis, under a title which the working press quickly and regrettably transformed from "A List of Great Books" to "The Hundred Great Books." It is a list that has been subject from the start to constant revision in the light of teaching experience.

A LIST OF GREAT BOOKS

Homer: *Iliad* and *Odyssey*
Aeschylus: *Oresteia*
Herodotus: *History*

Sophocles: *Oedipus Rex*
Hippocrates: Selections
Euripides: *Medea* and *Electra*
Thucydides: *History of the Peloponnesian War*
Old Testament
Aristophanes: *Frogs, Clouds, Birds*
Aristarchus: *On the Distance of the Sun and Moon*
Aristoxenus: *Harmony*
Plato: *Meno, Republic, Sophist*
Aristotle: *Organon* and *Poetics*
Archimedes: Works
Euclid: *Elements*
Appollonius: *Conics*
Lucian: *True History*
Plutarch: *Lives*
Lucretius: *On the Nature of Things*
Nicomachus: *Introduction to Arithmetic*
Ptolemy: *Almagest*
Virgil: *Aeneid*
Strabo: *Geography*
Livy: *History of Rome*
Cicero: *De Officiis*
Horace: *Ars Poetica*
Ovid: *Metamorphoses*
Quintilian: *Institutes*
Marcus Aurelius: *To Himself*
New Testament
Galen: *On the Natural Faculties*
Plotinus: *Enneads*
Augustine: *De Musica* and *De Magistro*
Song of Roland
Volsunga Saga
Bonaventura: *On the Reduction of the Arts to Theology*
Thomas: *Summa Theologica*
Dante: *Divine Comedy*

Roger Bacon: *Opus Maius*
Chaucer: *Canterbury Tales*
Leonardo: *Note-books*
Erasmus: *Colloquies*
Rabelais: *Gargantua*
Copernicus: *De Revolutionibus*
Machiavelli: *The Prince*
Harvey: *On the Motion of the Heart*
Gilbert: *On the Magnet*
Kepler: *Epitome of Astronomy*
Galileo: *Two New Sciences*
Descartes: *Geometry*
Francis Bacon: *Novum Organum*
Hobbes: *Leviathan*
Montaigne: *Essays*
Cervantes: *Don Quixote*
Shakespeare: *Hamlet, King Lear*
Calvin: *Institutes*
Grotius: *The Law of War and Peace*
Corneille: *Le Cid*
Racine: *Phèdre*
Molière: *Tartuffe*
Spinoza: *Ethics*
Milton: *Paradise Lost*
Leibniz: Mathematical Papers
Newton: *Principia*
Boyle: *Skeptical Chymist*
Montesquieu: *The Spirit of the Laws*
Swift: *Gulliver's Travels*
Locke: *Essay Concerning Human Understanding*
Voltaire: *Candide*
Fielding: *Tom Jones*
Rousseau: *Social Contract*
Adam Smith: *Wealth of Nations*
Hume: *Treatise of Human Nature*
Gibbon: *Decline and Fall of the Roman Empire*

Constitution of the United States
Federalist Papers
Kant: *Critique of Pure Reason*
Goethe: *Faust*
Hegel: *Science of Logic*
Schopenhauer: *The World as Will and Idea*
Coleridge: *Biographia Literaria*
Bentham: *Principles of Morals and of Legislation*
Malthus: *Essay on the Principles of Population*
Mill: *A System of Logic*
Marx: *Capital*
Balzac: *Père Goriot*
Thackeray: *Henry Esmond*
Dickens: *David Copperfield*
Flaubert: *Madame Bovary*
Dostoevsky: *Crime and Punishment*
Tolstoi: *War and Peace*
Zola: *Experimental Novel*
Ibsen: *The Doll's House*
Dalton: *A New System of Chemical Philosophy*
Clifford: *The Common Sense of the Exact Sciences*
Fourier: *Mathematical Analysis of Heat*
Faraday: *Experimental Researches into Electricity*
Peacock: *Algebra*
Lobachevski: *Theory of Parallels*
Darwin: *Origin of Species*
Mendel: Papers
Bernard: *Introduction to Experimental Medicine*
Galton: *Enquiries into the Human Mind and its Faculties*
Joule: *Scientific Papers*
Maxwell: *Electricity and Magnetism*
Gauss: Mathematical Papers
Galois: Mathematical Papers
Boole: *Laws of Thought*
Hamilton: *Quaternions*

Riemann: *Hypotheses of Geometry*
Cantor: *Transfinite Numbers*
Virchow: *Cellular Pathology*
Poincaré: *Science and Hypothesis*
Hilbert: *Foundations of Geometry*
James: *Principles of Psychology*
Freud: *Papers on Hysteria*
Russell and Whitehead: *Principia Mathematica*
Veblen and Young: *Projective Geometry*

The great books that appear in this list were written about many things, but they fall naturally into three main classes. Some of them picture men working, men choosing, men acting. These are the stories, the poems, the novels. Some of them seek to know the nature of things, whether of abstractions like number and magnitude or of the concrete things about us, a stick, a stone, a distant star, a tree, a horse, or even the living flesh of man. These are the mathematical and scientific works, and ultimately the metaphysical works as well. But there is a third group in this list of books. These last ask what a man ought to do. They deal with ethics, politics, economics. And some of them, instead of discussing the practical problems which all men must face, record how certain men once faced them. So the group includes histories and biographies, too.

The poet pictures men making choices. The scientist tries to understand the nature of the world in which those choices were made and in which future choices must be made. But these other authors deal inevitably with the burning question, What shall I choose? The poet offers us images that lead us towards beauty. The mathematician and the scientist distinguish ideas that lead us towards truth. But the authors I shall talk about here discuss human actions and ask which among these actions lead to the good. Their primary interest is not what is beautiful and what is ugly; it is not what is true and what is false; it is how to tell the good act from the bad. It is how to tell the good society from the bad. It is how to distribute those fruits of the earth that man gets in the sweat of his face.

What shall we call the authors of this third group? I hesitate to call them moralists. Whatever mistakes they made, they were certainly not guilty of what people now call moralizing. I hesitate to call them social scientists, because of certain connotations that this term now carries with it. For example, the last thing they would want to do is to make "value-free judgments." They themselves used to call their subjects the practical sciences, to distinguish them from the theoretical sciences. The theoretical sciences were concerned with the nature of things, regardless of human consequences. The practical sciences were concerned with what ought to be done. They were concerned not only with what the facts are, but with which facts ought to be; not only with what can be known, but with what ought to be desired; not only with true and false, but with right and wrong. If the reader will indulge me, I should like for the time being to call those authors who treated of such matters by their traditional name, practical scientists, as distinguished from natural scientists.

I do not doubt that the questions the practical scientists raise are, for the average reader, the most urgent questions that can be raised. This is not to underestimate the heavy problems the artist faces or the bewildering puzzles that confront the natural scientist. Poet, painter, sculptor, lie awake clutching at the elusive vision that seems just out of reach or grappling for the precise word, the precise color, the precise form, that will fix and communicate that vision. The natural scientist also spends his white nights trying to find the hidden meaning in the book of nature. But I suspect that, taking man by and large, the things that really pass through his sleepless mind or haunt his dreams when sleep has come at last are what to do about the friend he has wronged, where to find courage to face the thing he cannot dodge, how to steel himself against the lusts that deform his life and leave their telltale mark upon his very face. No unfinished poem, no bungled experiment, oppresses him, but fear, worry, frustration, gnawing doubt, fiery desire, greed, black hatred, the sense of guilt, shame, resentment, and despair. What he calls his personal life—it is this, and neither a poem nor a scientific hypothesis, that he has made a hash of. And it is precisely about these matters that the practical scientists talk. I expect, therefore, that he who reads them patiently will find the matter worth his reading time.

Ought I then to advise that reader who is neither poet nor physicist to choose out from these books the authors who deal with the practical matters that oppress us all, and leave the other books to quieter times than ours? It would be bad advice. To discover what is good or bad without worrying about what is true is not practicable and leads to the very type of "moralizing" that all of us justly hate. To try to discover the good act without having seen good men act, or the bad act without having seen bad men act, is to do things the hard way. It is to deal with abstractions without having any powerful images to lean on. It is to discuss courage without having stood beside Homer and watched the Achaeans do bloody battle on the dusty plain of Troy. Until we know the pale fear that seized their gleaming limbs, we risk having no full content for the word courage. Everybody, you say, has known fear, whether at Troy or elsewhere? At a minimum, Troy will bring back the violent memory of that fear. But, as a matter of fact, most people's experience has been sadly limited. And what there is of it has rarely been digested and understood. The poet furnishes us with the vivid image, the concrete example, the particular case, the perfect illustration, without which analysis constantly threatens to degenerate into verbalizing and logic-chopping. If we would measure the cost of intemperance, we must sit with the Trojan elders and watch Helen pass while the warriors fall like pine trees and their armor clangs about them. And how can most of us know the pang of watching those die whom we have led to their death unless we share Odysseus's agony as Scylla lifts six of his men from his ship, "they stretching forth their hands to me in the dread death-struggle. And the most pitiful thing was this that mine eyes have seen of all my travail in searching out the paths of the sea." [1] . . . And Hector's brother, smitten by Teucer's arrow, "bowed his head to one side like a poppy that in a garden is laden with its fruit and the rains of spring; so bowed he to one side his head, laden with his helmet." [2] Penelope at her web, Agamemnon pacing the purple robes to his doom, the vengeful Furies in full cry for the matricide Orestes, Oedipus's sudden comprehension that he has slain his father and begotten children by his mother, the relentless Medea seeking vengeance for desertion—these are the images, the memories, that Homer and the writers of the great tragedies can make a part of our experience.

Or how shall we fully plumb the depths of political folly unless we have laughed with Aristophanes at that wondrous state Cloudcuckooland? Or without watching Lysistrata organize a wives' strike against warrior husbands? Or without seeing Trygaeus off to heaven on his doodlebug steed in an effort to end war?

As with the epics, the tragedies, the comedies, so with the historians. If we would know war, we ought to watch with Herodotus while the followers of Xerxes scourge the blue waters of the Hellespont or while Xerxes, after reviewing his vast invasion forces, weeps that human life should be so brief. With Thucydides we should hear Pericles declare the Athenian state the school of Hellas, hear him describe the glory of Athens, and then watch the flight of the Athenian army before Syracuse. And if we would know what government is, we should observe, in Thucydides's laconic account of the revolution at Corcyra, what happens when it fails. If we would understand what a decision is, a choice, let Plutarch show us Alexander cutting the Gordian knot, or Caesar remembering his dream of incest with his mother and crossing the Rubicon to violate his mother Rome.

It is with these images that the great epics, tragedies, comedies, histories, and biographies fill out our meager personal experience to its full human dimensions and revive our withered imaginations. It is about such men and such acts that the practical scientists will be talking when they speak of moral choice or of citizenship or tyranny or anarchy. Without such acts, such scenes, such sufferings in mind, we shall not be in a position to measure the difficulties that confront a man who tries to think clearly and strongly about self-control or self-government; we shall not be able to measure his success or failure; often enough, we shall not even find a meaning in his words.

But if the poets and historians illumine the writings of moral and political thinkers, so do these writings reflect light back on the stories the poet tells. Unless we have struggled fruitfully with the problem of political authority, we risk seeing in the *Iliad* a quarrel between two conceited men about a woman seized for booty—and nothing more. We risk finding in the *Odyssey* a mere sailor's yarn. Homer, we will say blandly, was merely trying to tell a story. Why torture yourself looking for meanings in it? Don't read things into stories. Enjoy them.

Homer was indeed telling stories. But they are amazingly good stories. And if we examine our favorite anecdotes, we shall discover that the goodness of a story is not that it is good to eat, nor that it is good to wear, nor even that it will make some publisher rich. The goodness of a story is its significance.

To understand a story is to answer the question, What does it signify? It is to "read into" the story, not merely through it or over it. This is why the great books on morals and politics repay their debt to the poets and historians on whose stories they depend for the raw material of their conclusions. This is why any poet who scorns moral issues, who stakes all on Beauty, who thinks of himself as a fine-artist and hence exempt from moral or political responsibility, ends by knowing only the Pretty. He has failed to collect the debt the practical scientist owed him: he has failed to remember that the un-moral act is the merely animal act and hence not one of those acts most worth depicting. He has become a spoilt child, and trivial. It is this reciprocal action of the practical scientist upon the poet and of the poet upon the practical scientist that can contribute doubly to the reader's understanding if he reads the greatest authors of both groups.

For such reasons, then, the reader who would understand moral problems, political problems, economic problems, and even historical problems neglects the poets at his peril. But that is not all. He neglects also at grave peril the problems of mathematics and natural science.

Plato is said to have inscribed over the doorway of his Academy: "Let no man enter here who does not know geometry." Napoleon, military strategist and statesman, once remarked that the trouble with some of his contemporaries was that they needed a few lessons in geometry. All through Plato's writings runs the profoundest distrust of the "practical man"

whose practice is not grounded on clearly comprehended theory but only on luck and hunch. But
there runs also a belief that a man who cannot handle even the clean-cut abstractions of mathematics
will not likely be able to handle the much more
complicated abstractions of law and politics. Can the
concept of justice, without which law becomes a
travesty, ever be grasped by the man who cannot
even grasp the concept of triangularity or of propor-
tionality? That moral and political concepts should
be more difficult to apprehend than mathematical
ones can be explained simply enough. In the field of
morals and politics it is harder to be the disinterested enquirer. Note that I said "disinterested," not
"uninterested." One of the curses on our language
today is that the two have become possible synonyms.
The judge on the bench cannot follow a case if his
mind is uninterested in the case, but his judgments,
to be genuine judgments, must remain disinterested.
The uninterested man cannot see the problem, because his mind is not on it. The disinterested man
can see it, because only his mind—not his desires,
too—is on the problem. It is easier to be uninterested
in mathematics than in politics, because politics con-
cerns things we desire or fear while mathematics con-
cerns clean abstractions. But it is far, far easier to be
disinterested when enquiring into a mathematical
problem than when examining a political one, for
precisely the same reason. If we cannot handle abstractions where our fears and desires are unlikely
to deflect and contort our thought, how shall we
handle political problems well?

For Plato mathematics deals with ideas that are

permanent, not changing before our very eyes. And since the statesman, as distinguished from the mere politician, is also dealing with permanent considerations and how to apply them to a rapidly changing world of men and things, the statesman needs to have lived in the calm, clear world of mathematics before entering the confusing one into which his duties call him. But he needs to have lived in that clear world for another and more obvious reason. The government of men normally involves the government of things, and the industrial arts, through which we govern things, are in large measure based on mathematics. Most of our practical affairs involve also the physical welfare of persons, and this physical welfare depends on a knowledge of things. We need therefore to possess the theoretical sciences that unlock the secrets of the things we live amongst and daily use, including our own bodies.

For Aristotle the concepts he finds useful in physics—power and act, form and matter, change, causation—all have their analogous uses in the world of morals and politics. The power to assimilate food and to grow physically, which we share with plants and animals, is capped in man by a power to grow morally. Material objects change; an acorn changes into an oak. But political constitutions change, too. These things sound so familiar that they appear to be simple-minded when merely repeated flatly without the complications which such notions actually involve. But they may be worth stating here, even flatly, if only to suggest why the reader who would understand Aristotle's *Ethics* and his *Politics* will not be wasting time to read the *Physics,* too.

For the analysis of nature furnishes countless patterns for the analysis of practical affairs.

There are, then, two principal ways in which the great books that treat of mathematics and natural science directly contribute to our understanding of the great books that deal with practical human affairs. In the first instance, the former lead us into a field where we can more easily learn to analyze well, precisely because the issues under analysis are not confused by our own desires and prejudices. They are "safer" to discuss, and it is a safety that the newcomer to analysis badly needs. In the second instance, since practical affairs are dealt with in a world of measurable things, we ought to know how to measure and classify those things before trying to answer that haunting question, What ought I to do?

This debt that the practical sciences owe to the theoretical sciences will be repaid, as was the debt they owed to poetry. For it is the very nature of theoretical knowledge to ask itself what are its practical uses, and only the practical sciences can answer that question. Here is the formula for atomic energy. To what human uses should such energy be put?

I ask the reader's indulgence if I have too long labored the point. I have merely wanted to remind him of the grave dangers to human understanding that always lurk in an attempt to omit from our thinking whole fields of human thought. Scholars today generally boast of staying in their respective fields. For purposes of analysis a field of vision is a good thing, but only livestock will willingly stay always in respective fields. These books before us were written by great and daring thinkers who knew by how much men are more than livestock. These men who wrote them either decline flatly, when thinking and writing, to stay in a given field; or if they do stay in one, all that they say is charged with implications for all other fields as well. Their books are their signed invitations to us to quit, at least for a time, our special fields of interest and to dare to follow them on the high and open roads of human thought. On what proper grounds can we decline any one of these invitations?

To be quite candid, there are grounds for declining, though not adequate grounds. These high and open roads are covered with stones, and many travelers, after stumbling over a dozen or so, have gone back in disgust to their respective fields. These are the people who have ever since told us that they cannot read poetry or that they haven't got mathematical minds or that they don't understand politics and are not interested in morals. They are deceiving themselves; what they don't like is stones. And the stones on the high roads of human thought are chiefly terms.

Terms are words an author uses with a special meaning that he has purposely assigned to them to exclude other meanings which they may have elsewhere and to convey thereby his own special meaning more precisely. The existence of these terms gives a strange and unfamiliar ring to the great books of practical science, but they give the same ring to those on the theoretical, or natural, sciences and even to the great poets. Unfortunately, the terms in those works that treat of the practical are peculiarly subject to misunderstanding today. They are not merely not understood; they are misunderstood. Listen to them: good and evil, virtue and vice, right and wrong, duty, sin, desire, will, courage, temperance, justice, prudence, wisdom, morals, final end. To many readers today they have a Sunday-school smell, a smell of hypocrisy and cant. These are the ethical terms. The political terms are less offensive but they have become perhaps equally hazy: law, government, authority, sovereign, subject, aristocracy, monarch, peace, deliberation. But these terms are stumbling blocks only to the impatient reader who does not look where he puts his foot. All of them have exciting meanings—meanings that nobody who understands them and who is interested in these subjects would willingly dispense with.

Take "virtue," for example. Today, for many persons, it hardly means more than sexual abstinence. "Immorality" tends to mean merely sexual irregularity. "Morals" are thought of by the sophisticated as mores, manners, customs, by the simple-minded as sexual regularity. What were once called the cardinal virtues now have a hollow ring. "Courage" suggests heroics. "Temperance" sounds like the prohibition of alcoholic beverages. "Justice" is law-court stuff. And "prudence" involves life insurance and perhaps the Rock of Gibraltar. Yet, that the cardinal virtues are necessary if a man is not to be a mean rascal will be evident enough when I say that those who do not possess the cardinal virtues are cowardly, greedy, unfair, and foolish. Nobody really wants to be those things, not even the man who dislikes talk about virtue. Evidently, we are up against a problem of words. Yet "words are wise mens counters, they do but reckon by them: but they are the mony of fooles. . . ." This from Thomas Hobbes, and we must not be fooled by words if we would read wisely or well.

Nevertheless, so many of the words these authors use have degenerated with uncritical use by many mouths that I would willingly find the right modern synonyms, if I could. The brutal truth is that our thinking in the fields of morals and politics has of late been so irrelevant that the old traditional terms are the only names available for the things we shall be talking about. The modern terms, as a general rule, though less offensive to the modern ear, turn out to be not clear but fuzzy, where the old terms turn out at the last to be not fuzzy but clear. These terms are counters; let us reckon by them.

Finally, I shall imitate the faculty of St. John's College and revise their list to suit my present purpose. I shall speak of a few books that they did not include, or at least did not in 1937. Sometimes, I shall replace a book by another from the same pen, as in the case of Augustine and Freud. Once, I chose an author, Tacitus, who was not then on the list.

THE
DIALECTICAL
REPUBLIC

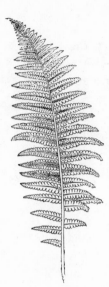

THE DIALECTICAL REPUBLIC

The great key works of the ancient world in the practical sciences are Plato's *Republic* and Aristotle's *Ethics* and *Politics*. To these should be added the *Charmides*, the *Laches*, the *Philebus*, the *Laws*, and indeed most of the other dialogues of Plato; and the works of the great Stoics Epictetus and Marcus Aurelius. In history, there are Herodotus, Thucydides, Tacitus; and in biography, Plutarch.

None of these writers wastes time being neutrally descriptive, or "value-free." They are normative. For them human life has purpose. It chooses out and employs means in order to achieve certain ends. To live requires intelligence and will. To consider one way of living as good as another, one way of governing a state as good as another, does not touch the problem. These authors assume that the reader's highly practical problem is, What shall *I* choose, personally and politically? The advice of Plato and Aristotle is not, of course, arbitrary. It is based on their view of what a man is. They say, in effect: "Given man's nature, if he wants to be happy, these are the means he must voluntarily select, these are the kinds of acts he must habitually perform." In Epictetus and Marcus Aurelius the advice gets even heavier.

Even the historians are not neutral. True, their job resembles the job of the theoretical scientist in that their prime concern is with truth. It resembles the poet's job in that their focus is on the particular man, the particular act, the particular time and place. But all historians stand on Thucydides' defense of his history, that "if it be judged useful by those enquirers who desire an exact knowledge of the past as an aid to the interpretation of the future, which in the course of human things must resemble if it does not reflect it, I shall be content." [3] They propose, in effect, to enlarge the practical experience of their reader in order that he may make wise decisions himself, both personal and political, in solving the practical problems that confront him today. They mean to be instructive, and for highly practical purposes.

Precisely because they propose to instruct where instruction is what the reader wants, they succeed in being often as moving as a poet, as rigorous in enquiry as a theoretical scientist. Similarly, the poet who holds fast to his job of telling a good story is often more instructive than a confused moralist. So is the theoretical scientist who never forgets his commitment to seek the truth, regardless of practical consequences. This is another aspect of the point I have already asked forgiveness for laboring: not only do the poet, the theoretical scientist, and the practical scientist throw light on each other's work; they actually do some of each other's work as an inevitable obligato to doing their own well. For seeing the beautiful, knowing the true, loving the good—these are the three ways of remaining completely alive.

Leaving aside the Bible, no other writer whose works have reached us ever lived in all three ways at once more surely than Plato in his *Dialogues*. The *Dialogues* are, therefore, not merely the model for all time of what good conversation ought to be— wise, witty, courteous, ironic, imaginative, serious, graceful, humorous, and never cheap or lazy or obvious. They are the works of a brilliant dramatic poet, of an intrepid seeker after objective truth, of one who loved the good in all things under the sun. Being alive in all three ways at once, Plato has always known how to attract and grip readers who are alive, or even half alive, in one of them. But he has also offended professors of philosophy by his jests; interrupted pedants with his lyric outbursts; frightened the literary critics with the rigor and abstractness of his thought; aroused the scorn or hatred of the cynics by his faith in man; and terrified the sentimentalists by his complete awareness of the less lovely side of human life.

The *Dialogues* purport to be conversations between Plato's great teacher, Socrates, and the disciples and critics of Socrates. Whether they "actually" occurred is irrelevant; they have occurred now. Plato saw to that. If the reader plans to write a life of Socrates, or one of Plato, he might profitably speculate on whether Plato remembered them or invented the *Dialogues*. Otherwise, he would better listen to what they say.

The *Dialogues* are dialectical. This sounds almost like saying that spheres are spherical, and it is indeed a little like saying that. It is more like saying that this particular sphere, unlike many spheres, is really spherical. A dialogue is a conversation, but not many conversations rise to the level of dialectic. In most conversations Jones expresses an opinion and then Smith expresses an opinion. If the two opinions are about the same subject but differ from each other, the conditions exist for dialectic. In real life they are sometimes not about the same subject, not even about distantly related subjects. In this fashion, Jones and Smith may go on for hours expressing unrelated opinions. All of us have heard them do it. This is not dialectic. Strictly speaking, it is not even a dialogue, not even a conversation. Two men are engaging in two separate monologues in each other's presence. Generally, Jones uses the time during Smith's speeches to compose his own next speech. Smith returns the compliment.

There is another situation, familiar to all of us, in which something a little more like dialectic occurs, a thing that Socrates called eristic. To engage in eristic, the opinions you start with must be about the same subject and again they must differ from each other. An argument begins. The object of the opponents is to "win the argument" whether or not they learn anything from it. The speakers tend to show off, to make each other look small, to cite authorities. They tend to grow angry, to talk loudly, and to make long speeches at each other. They tend to use trickery, though trickery is not a necessary feature of eristic. They will most likely tend to hold at the same opinions they started with, and will hold them more fiercely, and will suspect the morals of their opponent.

But out of the same initial situation can arise the thing Socrates calls dialectic. Although dialectic sounds to the uninitiated very like eristic, since both are arguments between opposing parties, it differs profoundly in intention and usually in result. In dialectic you choose sides, but the point of the game is to understand better: to understand your own opinion and the opinion of your opponent, and from the clash of opinion to rid yourself of false opinion and maybe to get a little knowledge. In order to do this, it is necessary to maintain your position stoutly but honestly. If you lose a point, you are glad to yield; because if something you thought true turns out to be untrue you have lost a piece of falsehood. You literally don't care who wins provided you and your opponent get rid of enough false opinions. When you lay a logical egg, no matter how good it looks, you never cackle, because it may always turn out to a wind-egg, as Socrates would call it—from which nothing living will ever be hatched.

A quick way to distinguish between monologuists pretending to converse, disputants practising eristic, and philosophers practising dialectic, is to think of three different things that can be done by two men on a tennis court. One thing would be for both men to drive all balls into the net or even against their respective backstops. This might develop their stroke, but it will prevent a game from even starting. Another thing would be for them to play a set by regular tennis rules and play with no other motive than to win. Each would rather win a set of badly played tennis than lose a set of excellently played tennis. One of them may cheat ever so little if necessary. It is not the tennis that interests him; it is the final score. This is the eristic method in tennis. A third thing would be for both players to play good, hard tennis, not greatly caring who may win, but determined that the play shall be skillful and hence exciting. This third way of using a tennis court would resemble dialectic.

I have lingered over the word dialectic because it is a key word in Plato's dialogue, *The Republic,* and because that dialogue is dialectical in two senses. In the first place, like most of the other Platonic dialogues, the conversation it records is a highly dialectical one. In reading it, we watch good dialectic being practised, the kind we ought to imitate. In the second place, Socrates in this conversation constructs an imaginary state, and the guarantee of good government that he offers is that the rulers of his state should be highly trained in dialectic.

Watching Socrates practise dialectic, not only in the *Republic* but in the other dialogues, we can note several important facts about him. He is convinced that while he knows nothing—except that he knows nothing—all too many men know nothing but think they know a great deal. That is, they hold many opinions which have not yet undergone the trial by dialectic, have not been submitted to rigorous examination. So far as my memory goes, there are only two other things that Socrates ever claims he knows, except this fact that he knows nothing. Once, in the dialogue called the *Meno,* he remarks: "Some things I have said of which I am not altogether confident. But that we shall be better and braver and less helpless if we think that we ought to enquire, than we should have been had we indulged in the idle fancy that there was no knowing and no use in seeking to know what we do not know; —that is a theme upon which I am ready to fight, in word and deed, to the utmost of my power." [4] Note that he "knows" this only by faith.

But he knows another thing and on this he testifies also in the *Meno:* "I too speak rather in ignorance; I only conjecture. And yet that knowledge differs from true opinion is no matter of conjecture with me. There are not many things which I profess to know, but this is most certainly one of them." [5] He disclaims possessing "the Truth," but he can see through the claims of those who think they do possess it. This, naturally, will irritate them vastly, and eventually they will indict him in court for atheism and for corrupting the youth, and sentence him to death. They cannot believe he is not giving himself airs. Nor, frequently, can the modern reader. "And I am called wise," he says a few minutes before he is condemned, "for my hearers always imagine that I myself possess the wisdom which I find wanting in others: but the truth is, O men of Athens, that God only is wise; . . ." [6] They imagine that Socrates either possesses the Truth, or claims to.

Finally, Socrates dislikes the appeal to authority and he dislikes people who try to own an idea. You cannot trust the truth of a statement by saying a wise man said it. Even wise men make foolish mistakes. Even fools sometimes have a good idea. For these reasons Socrates shows less respect for famous scholars than is usually considered polite and more respect for shoemakers and sailors than is usually considered necessary. Indeed, he is ready to respect anybody who is seeking, but nobody who is not seeking. In short, he respects those who "follow the argument whithersoever it leads," which is to say that he respects reason, and persons in so far as they are obedient to reason. No wonder he was executed.

He says that ever since childhood a voice within him has frequently warned him not to do things but has never told him what it is he ought to do. Set this beside the fact that the "Socratic method" of examining a problem through dialectic frequently tells him what opinions are no longer worth holding but never tells him "the Truth." But he knows there are things he ought to do; he knows that the truth exists; and this most peaceable of men will fight, intellectually and physically for one thing, the right and duty of the human mind to question—humbly, but question!

For thousands of readers the trial of Socrates has recalled the mock trial of Jesus of Nazareth. For thousands his patient acceptance of unjust execution has recalled the Nazarene. But I have never seen anywhere in print one of the most striking common features of these two teachers and of their doctrines. Jesus taught that if our enemy strikes us on one cheek, we must turn the other. I imagine no piece of advice he ever gave has been less heeded by his followers, from the time Peter cut off Malchus' ear down to the present. The dialectic of Socrates dramatically exemplifies the fruits of non-resistance to violence. If a man expresses a stupid opinion or even a personal insult, Socrates always accepts the opinion for purposes of immediate exploration and asks pardon of his insulter. In the same situation most of the rest of us jump down the throat of him who expresses the stupid opinion; or at a minimum, immediately express the opposite; and as for the insult, we think we have done well when we rebuke our opponent mildly for being personal. But Socrates does one more thing: in accepting insults and stupid opinions he uses not only formal courtesy but deep irony. In the first book of *The Republic,* where he deals successively with a rich and self-complacent old man and with a disputatious, vain, and brutal sophist, almost every remark he makes carries two meanings: one in case his interlocutor is not yet ready to examine himself, and the other for use at the very moment that the interlocutor sees his folly. His acts, like his words, are double; even his execution is loaded with irony for the men of Athens.

One day when Socrates was visiting the Piraeus, the port of nearby Athens, and was talking with friends at the home of a rich, elderly business man, the conversation turned to the nature of justice. Various members of the group tried to define it as paying one's debts, telling the truth, benefiting friends and injuring enemies, or as whatever results naturally from the brutal fact that might makes right. All these theories, under the questioning of

Socrates, were found to lead to contradictions or absurdities; they failed under ordeal by dialectic. Incidentally, Socrates forced the admission that contrary to popular opinion the just man, not the "successful" unjust man, is the happy man, and that it is actually better to be injured than to injure. But what justice is, seemed to remain a mystery.

Then Socrates suggested that it might be easier to locate justice in a politically organized society than in an individual, since a state is bigger than a man and might be expected to have a bigger piece of justice in it. Then if they could identify it in a state, they might by analogy locate it in the individual. For this purpose he undertook to build for them in imagination a perfect state, or Republic. Noting that somebody would have to defend it by force, both against foreign enemies and against civil disorder, he assigned that duty to a warrior class. Since this state must also be governed, he chose from among his warriors a smaller class of "guardians," whom the rest would serve as obedient "auxiliaries." The remaining citizens, whether laborers, craftsmen, or merchants, would be responsible for the production and distribution of commodities. He then discovered that the class that especially needed courage would be the professional army, the auxiliaries. Temperance or self-control, the next virtue men commonly talked about, would take the form of obedience to the guardians both by the auxiliaries and by the producers. Wisdom would be especially required by the guardians, who were responsible for making the laws and governing the whole state. The remaining cardinal virtue, justice, must consist, he thought, in each class performing its proper function and not trying to usurp the function of one of the other classes.

To make sure that the guardians would govern wisely, he forbade them to own private property, since such property would make them less disinterested in their decisions. He even insisted, with apologies for the strange idea, that they must share their wives and children so that they might not be tempted to substitute family interest for the public interest. Their children were bred eugenically to get the best raw material for the guardian class, and that raw material was subjected to a long and rigorous education to develop its intellectual powers to the utmost. Even when all that was done, Socrates pointed out, such a state would never likely exist on this earth; it would remain a pattern laid up in heaven by which to judge the quality of actual states here below; and even if it did come into existence here, it would degenerate in terms of its central purpose from wisdom to honor, from honor to money-making, from money to license disguised as liberty, and finally to the blackest tyranny.

By analogy with the state, Socrates and his friends now located in the individual the virtue of justice, which they had been seeking, and the other cardinal virtues as well. Courage is to be found in the "spirit" or aggressive drive in a man when properly subordinated to reason, as the auxiliaries should be properly subordinate to the guardians. Temperance is that subordination itself, which in the individual, reason exacts from spirit and from the lower physical appetites, those appetites that attend to the "economy" of a man, the maintenance of his physical body. And the wisdom, that in the case of the state resides primarily in the guardians, in the individual resides in the intellect. The proper functioning, in relation to each other, of intellect, spirit, and appetites is the virtue men call justice. Moreover, to each type of man corresponds a type of government. To the best and wisest type of man corresponds "aristocracy," rule by the best and wisest citizens in a given state, the very type of government Socrates had just finished imagining. To the next best type, the soldier and "man of honor," corresponds timocracy, government by honor, where in effect the auxiliaries have deposed the guardians and where the individual has, to use a current colloquialism, "the right attitude" without knowing why it is right. To the third best type of government, "oligarchy," or government by the few and richest, corresponds the prudent, careful business man who exercises self-control in his pleasures, because he respects material things and considers it, therefore, sinful to waste them. The next type of government is a libertarian, egalitarian democracy, in which everybody who can, follows his whims without recognizing any higher sanction— even the oligarch's sanction of thrift—and where difference in quality is ignored or denied, and where both respect for others and self-respect disappear. Finally, from this disorderly and childish society tyranny arises and is reflected in the character of the man whose reason is completely enslaved by his passions.

These are some of the things that Socrates and his

friends talked about that day at the Piraeus, according at least to Plato's great dialogue *The Republic.* But I have given only the bare bones of a living and vital discussion, which is perhaps the most brilliant single conversation ever recorded between human beings. Because the Republic that Socrates poetically portrays is governed by a few, it has been denounced by modern democrats as fascism; but the denunciation is based on a fundamental misunderstanding. Fascism glorifies violence. Plato glorifies reason. His *Republic* is at once a treatise on ethics and a treatise on politics and revolves appropriately around the most essentially social of the cardinal virtues, justice. But to know justice and to follow it, one must reason well, and according to *The Republic,* the guardians can reason adequately only by the most strenuous cultivation of their intellectual powers. It is in the discussion, therefore, of the education of the guardians that we will again meet the necessity for dialectic.

The early education of the young consists of music and gymnastic. By music Socrates means not only what we mean, but poetry as well. By gymnastic he means not only sports but all that will develop the perfect co-ordination of the bodily powers. Gymnastic will make the young tough and courageous. Music—and it has to be very carefully chosen music —will render their minds pliable and receptive to ideas. For poetry and music introduce through the senses, before the intellect has as yet been highly developed, the harmonies and relationships that can later be seen intellectually and abstractly. Poetry and music show forth in image what can later be grasped as idea.

Next comes a strenuous course of mathematics: arithmetic, plane and solid geometry, a quite different kind of "music"—this kind more like our mathematical physics—and astronomy. All these subjects have practical applications, but it is not because they are practical that Socrates wants his young men and women to study them. It is precisely in order that they may learn to handle abstractions, ideas, principles, as distinguished from their concrete embodiments in the objects around them. He wants them to discover that the "mind's eye" can see more clearly and more surely in the world of ideas than the body's eye can in the world of visible objects. He is trying to raise them from the physical world, in which all animals move, to the intellectual world, in which only the human animal can move and in which most human animals to date have learned to move only haltingly and very clumsily and very incredulously.

Once the students have mastered the four mathematical sciences, sciences that will some day come to be numbered among the seven liberal arts, the ablest among them will embark on dialectic. In mathematics they assumed the first principles of science, such as the axioms of geometry, as being self-evident and not subject to investigation. In dialectic they will investigate these assumptions, and explore the assumptions that lie back of them, and the assumptions that lie back of those assumptions. In short, they will be trained in metaphysics. In his allegory of "the divided line" at the end of Book VI and in his allegory of "the cave" at the beginning of Book VII Plato shows us Socrates hesitantly, modestly, reverently, expounding the fruits of this high discipline. His exposition strains the credulity of the average reader in much the same way that an exposition of nuclear physics would strain the credulity and try the patience of a healthy child who held that seeing is believing, and who could not yet see with the mind's eye. It is at the end of many years of this strenuous intellectual discipline, that the guardians may be entrusted with the practical responsibilities of government. But unlike present-day political candidates, says Socrates, they will not now be blind seekers after power. Their desires will be fixed on the vision of the Good, which after long practice in ascending and descending dialectic (induction and deduction, as we now say), these guardians may come to intuit directly. Other goods they will desire only as they resemble, reflect, and lead to this supreme Good. However, they will not be allowed to withdraw permanently to a contemplative life, for each must serve his tour of duty in the government.

What Plato has done in *The Republic,* among many things, is to write a treatise on ethics and at the same time a treatise on political science, and in doing so to produce a literary masterpiece of imperishable beauty. He has furnished us tests for judging whether a man is good, and whether a state is good. His answer in each case is, When obedience to reason has become the constant guide of practical action; when through arduous and apparently "impractical," "irrelevant," but truly liberal education, a man has developed the power to distinguish means from ends; and when the real good, rather than the apparent good, is freely and intelligently chosen.

Such an individual, as he explains at greater length in the *Laches,* will have courage because he will know what ought to be feared and what ought not to be feared. He will have temperance because physical pleasures cannot blind his reason and because he understands the reasons, as set forth in the *Philebus,* for distrusting pleasure and pain as guiding principles. He will be just because his reason rules him. And he will be wise because he has learned to live in the permanent world of ideas and to refer back to that world for guidance when he must act in the changing and imperfect world of things. If the human virtues are not, quite simply and flatly, knowledge—a point excitingly debated in the *Meno*—at least they depend directly on it. Plato is skeptical when we say we did a thing even though we knew it was wrong. No man, Socrates keeps repeating, knowingly chooses evil. It was because we were not so sure as we now think we were about the wrongness of the thing we did, that we went ahead and did it. The cure for vice, the cure for cowardice, greediness, crookedness, and folly, is knowledge.

Similarly, if we would live in a good society, then this society must be governed by those who have learned to love, and constantly to seek, knowledge and wisdom; it must not be governed by the ambitious, the blind seekers after power. It must be defended by brave and skilful armed forces with a high sense of honor and of obedience to the government. It must be served by producers and distributors aware that they are neither statesmen nor soldiers. And citizens must be chosen for these respective occupations by those most able to choose well. These are the basic functions of any organized state. No state can exist without them, and no state can serve the political needs of a truly good man unless these functions remain clearly-defined and clearly-related. There will be peace, order, and freedom in such a state. Such a state, to borrow from the phrase which Thucydides ascribed to Pericles, will be essentially a school. It will provide essentially for a learning society, and therefore a society that is growing morally, that is becoming constantly less childish and more adult. In any other sort of state the truly good man will find no genuine scope. He is likely to be "unsuccessful," scorned, hated, feared, and perhaps killed. Or worse still, from Plato's point of view, society may corrupt him and make him over in its own image.

Precisely because Plato's ideal Republic appears to be anti-democratic, to be governed by a class, and to employ censorship unblushingly, the modern reader is likely to overlook its deepest characteristic: it is a dialectical state. This, if understood, ought to endear it to the liberal. Every device in it is aimed at making sure that enquiry shall be continuous and of the best quality. Only a clear, hard theoretical grasp of the good of a society will keep statesmanship from degenerating into cheap politics. At the very pinnacle of government there is arduous study, study which sounds, as Plato describes it, more like the contemplation of Yogis than like the carefree life of an American school or college. And if the modern reader dislikes Yogis and even distrusts the word contemplation, he might well remember that he himself would be distrusted in the same way, in his more thoughtful moments, by almost any active, restless child. Plato's ideal Republic is even a highly competitive society with a career wide open to talent, although the competition is of a more significant character than the business competition we praise today. Part of the "justice" that permeates Socrates' imaginary Republic is the prompt promotion or demotion of citizens who have not yet found their true function in society.

It is true that since the dialectic practised by the guardians is a strenuous art, involving a long and difficult preparation, not every citizen can engage in it. In so far as Plato discusses the education of those who are neither auxiliaries nor guardians, it would appear to be largely aesthetic and unconscious in character. There is no shred of evidence that he was uninterested in their education, and even less that he wanted to prevent their fullest possible development. But the clash of opinion and the means of thorough deliberation are the very mainspring of government. Political and economic policy would be the fruit of that constant and rigorous debate.

Not only, one must add, does growth of knowledge at the peak of government serve to guide practical affairs. The wise solution of practical problems at the bottom is the means of this growth of knowledge. Starting out with a state that men find necessary if there is to be enough division of labor to guarantee their physical existence, Plato ends with a division of opinion that will guarantee their intellectual existence. We human beings need to dwell together, if we would help each other to eat; but we should dwell in such a way that we can help each other also to think. It is as if Socrates, who so loved conversation whenever he could force it up to a dialectical level, had devised a state capable of keeping good conversation going!

A generation of Americans that has made the word "dialogue" a somewhat painful cliché ought certainly to applaud Socrates for attaching so much importance to it, or at least to the kind of dialogue he called dialectic. But, alas, this kind is difficult to learn, if only because it sorely wounds the ego of the beginner. For it requires the power to think rigorously, and few of our contemporaries, even those on campuses, wish to do that. In fact, many of them openly abhor thinking, abhor the abstractions that those who would govern Plato's Republic must learn to handle with ease, grace, and pleasure. Many of our undergraduates do not wish to think but to "feel," as if those "guardians" of the Republic whom Socrates so eloquently described felt no ecstasy of the sort he says they felt.

I do not know of any major idea in Aristotle's *Ethics* and *Politics* that is not implicit in Plato's *Republic,* but it is Aristotle's genius to make these ideas explicit. For the poetic insight of *The Republic* he substitutes a shrewd and profound analysis. So magnificent a job has he done that his language has become the common-sense language we daily speak, and this may lead the unwary reader to find him commonplace and unoriginal. Characteristically, he divides off ethics from political science and focuses on them one at a time.

A virtue, says Aristotle, is a habit. It is a habit of action, not of blind action but of deliberate, voluntary action. To possess the virtue of courage it does not suffice to perform one brave act. Single, or occasional, brave acts have been performed by cowards. The truly brave man habitually does the courageous thing after examining in advance and then freely and gladly choosing the consequences of the act. So with the virtue of self-restraint, or temperance. So with justice. These habits are acquired, like all human habits, through practice and repetition. If you would be habitually brave, perform a courageous act and keep on performing such acts, no matter how much effort it costs you, until courageous action is natural to you; until it is, as we say, "second nature." When you have acquired all the moral virtues, you will have changed your "character," your *ethos*.

Man, for Aristotle, in common with all other beings possesses by nature certain powers. Like plants, he has a natural power to assimilate food and grow. Like other animals, he has the powers of sense perception and of locomotion. But unlike them, he has also the powers of reason and hence the power to act under the guidance of reason. When a man does it, he has "actualized" that power. But if he repeats the act often enough, his power to act a certain way occasionally and with difficulty has been actualized into power, or capacity, to act that way easily, gracefully, and pleasurably. The acquisition of a virtue, therefore, is like the acquisition of an artistic skill. I have the power to play a piano, in that as a normal human being I could learn to do it, though I have not yet learned and therefore could not play the piano this evening. If I did learn, I would possess the power or capacity in a new sense, ready for immediate use. Learning to be a piano player, then, will consist of a series of actualizations of my powers at various stages of learning. Becoming a good man, that is, a man who possesses the moral virtues of courage, temperance, justice, and prudence, is a process of turning power into act. By his nature a man could become a good man. Once he has become good, now by his developed character he can perform good acts, even if he is not performing one at this moment, even if at this particular moment he happens to be sleeping.

These moral virtues are habits of the will, which in turn is that power of the intellect that can love the good and choose it. But the intellect is concerned not only with what is good but with what is true and with what is beautiful. In its search for truth it has the power to act in various ways, and these powers also can through repeated acts become habits or virtues. These are the intellectual virtues as distinguished from the moral virtues, and Aristotle lists them. Art, he says, is the habit of making things well—a statue, a chair, a cloak. Prudence, or "practical wisdom," is the habit of skilfully choosing the right means for the right ends. Since no moral act, whether of justice, temperance, or courage, can be performed without the guidance of prudence, prudence is often classed among the moral virtues, too. Science, or the power of demonstration, is the developed power of deducing from the antecedent the necessary consequent, of passing from premise to conclusion. Intuition is the power to understand directly, without demonstration. It is the power used in induction, when we see in a flash the general principle behind the particular case. Philosophic wisdom is a combination of science and intuition. It is the intellect's highest faculty, or capacity.

Let us list them again, for they are of enormous importance to Aristotle's view of the moral problem: art, or technical skill; prudence, or practical wisdom, the power of choosing the right action; scientific knowledge, the power to demonstrate, to know what "follows," to follow an argument; intuition, the power of seeing the general in the particular, and of seeing the first principles from which demonstration can be made; and philosophic wisdom, in which intuition and science combine to produce the highest of these five "intellectual virtues."

It will be obvious that the moral virtues depend on these intellectual virtues, and most immediately on the border-line virtue of prudence or practical wisdom. This dependence is what led Socrates to raise the question in the *Meno* of whether, indeed, virtue was not essentially knowledge; although he is troubled by the fact that the moral virtues are not easily taught, whereas knowledge is essentially teachable. But it is also true that the intellectual virtues cannot be acquired in any high degree by a man who

fails to possess the moral virtues. This reciprocal connection between the good habits of the human
character and the good habits of the human intellect is connected with the metaphysical connection of
the true and the good. It accounts for Socrates's
awareness that the guardians cannot be trusted to
decide on what is good or bad for society unless they
are constantly concerned with what is true or false.
Yet if they rise high enough through dialectic in
their search for the true, what shines out at the sum-
mit of their climb is the Good. The connection between Aristotle's two sets of virtues will also account
for Socrates's provisions for the training of the young.
They will have been practising the moral virtues for
many years before they are allowed to begin their
training in mathematics, let alone dialectic. Only
the good man thinks really well. Only the man who
thinks well and skilfully can be truly good in any
important sense. It is these difficult problems that
lie back of our debate today as to whether education
ought to be concerned with the training of character
or with the development of the mind. Plato and
Aristotle seem to reply that character training, apart
from the development of the intellect, is appropriate
for puppies but not for men. Yet men cannot fully
become men until they have learned to think well,
and they cannot learn to do this until they have good
characters. Then men's characters should be moulded
when they are most like puppies; that is, when they
are young. They should be taught when they are
children to act without much deliberate choice the
way a virtuous man acts from deliberate choice.
When they have acquired the intellectual virtues,

they will discover why they were taught to act in that fashion and will knowingly choose to act so.

One last consideration. For Aristotle, even more definitely than for Plato, man's highest happiness is that he function as man, that he realize himself, that he actualize his human powers. But his highest powers Aristotle finds in his capacity for philosophic wisdom. Theoretical thinking, contemplation, is therefore the activity which most completes and perfects him. It is the activity most like God's activity and most draws man to God. This is the happiness the guardians of Plato's Republic knew, and its highest reaches are a kind of ecstasy.

To such a creature, to such a half-divine animal, must a good state conform. In the *Ethics* Aristotle first collects commonly held opinions before he attempts to extract from their confusion and self-contradiction a consistent theory of moral conduct and its goal, happiness; so in the *Politics* he first discusses existing states, their constitutions, their successes and failures, before he attempts in the last two books of his treatise to analyze the ideal state. The *Politics,* like the *Ethics,* exhibits little of the exquisite beauty of literary form which Plato infused into his *Dialogues,* partly because the manuscripts are in less good condition (the last part of the *Politics* is indeed missing entirely) and partly because what does exist is sometimes patchwork and may indeed consist of students' notes on Aristotle's lectures. But the close observation and acute analysis would by themselves rescue these two treatises from mediocrity.

As in *The Republic,* and for the same reasons, one of the state's most vital functions is education. For, like Plato, Aristotle is interested not merely in those functions of the state which are necessary to the citizen's physical existence, such as protection from violence and a division of labor to facilitate production and distribution, but in the ways in which a state enables the individual man to realize his highest powers, his intellectual powers. A state, to be good, must facilitate the citizen's acquisition of the moral and intellectual virtues. For the highest purpose of the state is human happiness.

Although Aristotle insists more explicitly than Plato that education must be universal, he scandalizes us by his cool acceptance of human slavery not only as necessary but as just. Although his argument is illuminating and should spur us to examine more critically in what sense all men are equal, it is not convincing even in terms of Aristotle's own political philosophy. His defense of slavery could lend small comfort to any actual slave system that ever existed, because of his sharp distinction between the man who is merely a legal slave through personal misfortune and the man whose incapacity to direct his own life towards happiness fits him only to help another achieve happiness. The latter, he declares, is a "slave by nature." One suspects that, because he was convinced that those with least native capacity could with most justice carry on whatever of society's work requires least capacity, he was misled into consoling himself with the belief that they were a sort of half-men anyway. On the other hand, if shuttles could weave cloth automatically, he observes, there would be no need for slaves. Are men slaves because they are only half-men, or because we lack automatic shuttles? Before we condemn Aristotle for thinking badly, we might note that with no machine production available, the least capable either had to serve at a low economic level or run the risk that no political order might emerge, in which case they would exchange humble membership in a civilized society for anarchy.

This slip of Aristotle's on slavery, if it is a slip, is not unconnected with the fact that *oikonomia,* from which words like economics and economy are derived, means primarily household management. The economic bases of a good society are mere means to the political end, as political science deals with mere means to an ethical end. Aristotle therefore, like Plato, deals sketchily with economics, although he is quite aware that the quickest way to get rich is to seize a monopoly. And he is interested in the general economic conditions that make a good society possible.

Both Plato and Aristotle assume war as an inevitable function of the state. In *The Republic,* it is true, Socrates hints that it is a high standard of living that introduces war, since the origins of war are economic. And Aristotle hints in the *Politics* that wars between the Greek states might be obviated by a unity of constitutions. But basically both regard war as a necessary evil.

Now the two greatest histories that have come down to us from ancient Greece are histories of wars: the history of the Persian Empire's unsuccessful invasions of Greece, by Herodotus, and the history of the Peloponnesian War, by Thucydides. Both histories are mines of exemplary materials for the problems Plato and Aristotle dealt with, but this would be less true were it not that both historians write of men as moral and political agents. Neither is insensitive to man as animal, moved by animal passions, by greed, the lust for power, unreasoning hates and fears. Neither is ignorant, therefore, of the tremendous role which economic interest plays in fomenting war and in guiding its course. But neither ever views man as merely an animal, albeit a shrewd animal. Though destiny and the intervention of the gods play their role, the history of Herodotus is a paean to political liberty successfully defending itself against the massed forces of tyranny, of men risking, or proudly giving, their lives that they or their children might live under law. That the Spartan dead who fell at Thermopylae move us so deeply is because they freely chose death. In the same way, Pericles's funeral oration over Athens's fallen soldiers, as reported by Thucydides, portrayed the good life and the political institutions that made a good life possible; and the oration still rings in our ears when Pericles has died and the folly and injustice of the Athenians mount and destruction comes upon them at Syracuse. Both histories achieve high significance because, in both, men are moved by ideas as well as by appetites. Neither of them spares us the sight of human folly, but neither is afraid to record human heroism, and neither is in doubt as to which is which. Both histories are rich in irony, heavy with tragedy, and free of cheap partisanship.

Both are genuinely dialectical in setting forth a conflict, not merely of men, but of ideas concerning what a man ought to do. Both therefore compel us who read them to fight in both armies. Because Persia stood for peace and order and law, we tread Xerxes's bridge across the Hellespont in the footsteps of his Immortals. And because men need freedom and the right to choose, we stand fast against Xerxes at Thermopylae and desert our Athenian homes for the ships off Salamis, bending our oar for freedom's sweet sake. Because, to quote Pericles, we judge "happiness to be the fruit of freedom and freedom of valor," we can face the Spartan heavy infantry. And because Athens everywhere is subjecting other states in the name of democracy, we will put to sea with the unskilled Spartan sailors and face the terrors of a skilled Athenian fleet, that Athenian imperialism shall not undo the deed done at Thermopylae. We are, and must be, on both sides, because ideas are on both sides, along with men willing to die for ideas. Not even the laughter of Aristophanes, moved by the absurdities of war, can furnish us with a pat and comfortable solution. For cowardice and greed and folly and deceit marched with both armies, too.

Plato and Aristotle view human life always in terms of purpose. So did Herodotus and Thucydides. For these men held that practical action, whether in the sphere of personal morals and personal happiness or in the field of politics and the good society, must serve the good of the intellect. The world of visible and tangible things mirrored a world open only to the mind, or intellect, of man. Man's task is to perfect, or complete, his nature; to perfect, above all, the intellectual part of his nature. Back of this recipe for action lies a metaphysical view of the nature of the universe. It is a universe of form and matter, of soul and body, of ideas and things, of eternity and time, of the unchanging and the ceaselessly changing, of being and becoming. Already in Aristotle we get the beginning of protest, in this case a protest that the idea as separated from its embodiment is taken by Plato as too real. Yet the Aristotelian man, like the Platonic man, can find happiness only in contemplation—even if he needs more material goods than the Platonic man to make his happiness genuine.

That metaphysical view was to disappear. In Lucretius we find a universe composed exclusively of solid atoms. Aristotle could discover four kinds of causation when he looked, for example, at a bronze statue. There was the material cause, the matter—in this case, bronze—from which it was made and without which it could not come to be. There was the efficient cause, the hand and the tools of the man who made it, the sculptor. There was the formal cause, the form or image or idea, the blueprint as it were, in the sculptor's mind. And there was the final cause, the purpose for which the statue was made. For Lucretius the only cause of anything is the matter. Out of a chaotic swirl of atoms was born all that we see about us, including our own bodies, including our own souls. For the soul, too, is made of atoms, although atoms of smaller size. Lucretius would have had a nasty time defending his Epicurean materialism in conversation with Socrates. Incidentally, because of this very materialism, Socrates would have censored Lucretius's poem *Of the Nature of Things* right out of the ideal Republic. The surpassing beauty of the imagery of that poem would merely have made it the more dangerous. For if Lucretius fumbled metaphysics, he did not fumble beauty. His great desire was to rid men of religion, of superstition, of the notion of divine intervention, of divine punishment, that they might revel in this material beauty without bothering their heads. There is no purpose in the universe; all is blind chance.

This metaphysical view enabled Lucretius to see, not the robust, brilliant, tragic world that Homer saw, but a pleasant, comfortable, melancholy place. It is a place that Virgil sees too in his epic poem, *The Æneid*. For like Lucretius, he is more interested in the practical than he is in the theoretical. Both poems are heavily moral, although the moralizing has not yet reduced great beauty to prettiness. Virgil shows us how a powerful, if somewhat uninspired, empire came into being; Lucretius shows us how to achieve a somewhat middle-aged happiness in such a state.

They would not have had to be their own metaphysicians and their own moralists, had better ones been available to support them and to free them for the task of hymning the results. Even Plutarch, superb biographer that he is, could have risen higher, had he, too, had the same intellectual supports. But what was still available is expressed by Epictetus and Marcus Aurelius, a slave and an emperor, both of whom saw the world as Stoics. The record of what they saw includes some of the most moving pages ever written; but the same melancholy suffuses those pages that suffuses the poems of Lucretius and Virgil.

Much had happened to the Mediterranean world since Plato and Aristotle wrote, and the essence of that much is recorded in the *Annals* and *History* of Tacitus. Those dark and gloomy and magnificent narratives portray the collapse of political liberty, the confused and sordid violence that repeatedly racked the Roman Empire, the vice that poisoned it. This is the tyrannical state that Socrates pictured with horror in *The Republic*, occasionally rescued, but only briefly, by some precursor of Marcus himself upon the imperial throne. Are the virtues of a good man, asked Socrates, the same as the virtues of a good citizen? Not, the Stoic must reply, in a state where true citizenship is a thing of the past. Even Socrates had found the Athens of his day a state in which he might teach but in which he could not run for office with any hope of bettering affairs. But he had faith that a pattern of the good city was laid up in heaven, a pattern "which he who desires may behold, and beholding, may set his own house in order. But whether such an one exists, or ever will exist in fact, is no matter; for he will live after the manner of that city, having nothing to do with any other." [7]

The Stoic's determination to live in accord with "nature" is akin to Socrates's determination, but it turns out to be a pale reflection of it. Less pale is the noble insistence of the Stoic that the whole human race are brothers. "If our intellectual part is common," writes Marcus Aurelius, "the reason also, in respect of which we are rational beings, is common: if this is so, common also is the reason which commands us what to do, and what not to do; if this is so, there is a common law also; if this is so, we are fellow-citizens; if this is so, we are members of some political community; if this is so, the world is in a manner a state. For of what other common political community will any one say that the whole human race are members?" [8]

This is a moralist's view of the political problem, and it is a high and generous and admirable view so far as it goes. Where it does not go is into the realm of theory and speculation which Plato and Aristotle alike sought as the true goal of man. By being merely practical, the Stoic's political theory is not practical enough.

Epictetus shared Marcus's neglect of philosophic theory: "The first and most necessary department of philosophy deals with the application of principles; for instance, 'not to lie'. The second deals with demonstrations; for instance, 'How comes it that one ought not to lie?' The third is concerned with establishing and analyzing these processes; for instance, 'How comes it that this is a demonstration? What is demonstration, what is consequence, what is contradiction, what is true, what is false?' It follows then that the third department is necessary because of the second, and the second because of the first. The first is the most necessary part, and that in which we

must rest. But we reverse the order: we occupy ourselves with the third, and make that our whole concern, and the first we completely neglect. Wherefore
we lie, but are ready enough with the demonstration
that lying is wrong." [9]

To a generation as anti-metaphysical, as anti-
intellectual as our own, this is persuasive talk. But
Socrates could have made as short work of this simple prescription as he did of the over-simplified accounts his friends gave him of the nature of justice.
In Socratic terms, this is to live by right opinion, not
knowledge. That is the way children must live; it is
not good enough for grown-ups. When grown-ups
try it, morals soon degenerate into mores. Then:
"When in Rome, do as the Romans do." Finally:
follow your unexamined desires.

By not fighting, with Socrates, for the right and
duty to enquire, by not wanting enough to know,
quite aside from what rules of conduct would follow
from knowing, the Stoic's morality as well as his
politics grew tight, constricted, oppressive, and
strained. He saved dignity, but lost joy, in his acts.
He refrained from joining the reckless grown-up
children who screamed about him, striving for bau-
bles, worrying over trifles, hurrying nowhere. But
he could offer the grown-up children nothing sufficiently better to call them from their nursery. At
best he gained tranquillity; at worst he could always
bow himself out. Socrates condemned suicide as
cowardice, and in the *Laws* provided that no suicide
should receive honorable burial. But Epictetus en-
visaged suicide as a possible way out, if life should
get too intolerable. Do not love too much, that you

may not suffer too much the loss of the loved one. Do not strive too much, in order that you may not suffer defeat. Here is a way for bearing with dignity a life that in very truth we find no longer tolerable. It asks less of life than perhaps a man should ask. After living for a few hundred pages in the world of Tacitus, it is easy to convince oneself that not too much could be asked. It is a weary and disillusioned world and its glance is backwards and regretful.

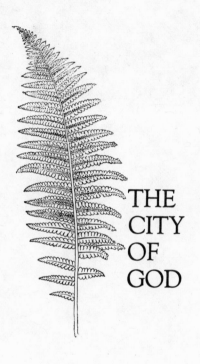

THE
CITY
OF
GOD

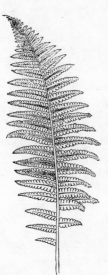

THE
CITY
OF
GOD

What must I do to find happiness? Plato answers that we must submit our bodily desires to the sweet rule of reason. Knowledge, and particularly self-knowledge, is our surest path. Sin is basically ignorance: no man wittingly chooses evil. The body is a prison of the soul, unless intellect learns to rule it. To choose the good, we must know the good. And this requires long and arduous self-discipline. Above all we must enquire. If our enquiry goes far enough, we shall see the Good itself. In the light of that vision, choice becomes clear.

Aristotle adds that good action depends largely on habits of the will. The soul can habituate the body to obedience; the recalcitrant matter in us can be moulded painfully towards supporting, instead of obstructing, our true purpose. That purpose, which for all men is happiness, can be found only in our highest activity, contemplative thought, in which we may know briefly the ecstasy that most likens us to God.

Lucretius the Epicurean tries to free us from the

fear of what may follow death by assuring us that nothing follows it. The universe is matter, unguided except by chance, and we ourselves are matter. Such a universe may be enjoyed, provided we do not strain after the impossible.

Epictetus and Marcus Aurelius the Stoics decline Plato's challenge to explore the invisible world of forms, of ideas. But they agree on constant self-examination. Do your duty. Study what is in your power and what is not in your power. What is in your power calls for wise practical action; what is not, is none of your business, and you will be a fretful child to worry about it. Learn to suffer and accept, as adults must. Accept the laws of nature. Discipline your will. In the Stoics's world there is not much room for love, but there is ample place for dignity. There is not much need for speculation, but there is a constant concern for morality.

But what if a man cannot refrain from loving? What if he be violent, passionate, brilliant, restless? What if he be born, a North African provincial, in the decaying society of the late Roman world? What if his youthful habits be formed by this society? What if he revels in its dissolute morals? What if, simultaneously, his restless mind should half descry the world of Plato's forms? And what if his love of both worlds drive him in two directions at once, until his divided will threatens to tear his heart and soul asunder?

These things happened to Augustine, who in the evening of his life made his *Confessions* to God in the hearing of us all. The book is the story of his conversion to Christianity and of what that conver-

sion cost him in agony of spirit. It is a tumultuous
story, written in tumultuous prose that rises in passage after passage to the height of great lyric poetry.
Although it often talks of the things that Plato talks
of, that invisible world seen only by the mind's eye,
it is couched in almost violent imagery. For Augustine was a sensualist before ever he became a saint.
The fierce delight of the flesh, the smells of Car-
thage, the taste of good food, the sound of music,
and the sight of shape and color had all goaded on
the young professor of rhetoric. Now they crowd to
his pen to help him, and us, ascend to Plato's world
of "forms."

There is nothing novel about Augustine's fundamental problem. In dialogue after dialogue of
Plato's, Socrates describes the bitter bondage of the
man who is enslaved to the desires of his body, who
wishes to escape from that bondage but cannot.
What is new is the incarnation of Jesus Christ, God
choosing to become man for the precise purpose of
redeeming man from that bondage.

It would be hard to imagine a greater paradox
than the incarnation of Jesus Christ. If we know
what the Old Testament meant by the word man,
then to say that God became a man—while remaining God—is, as Augustine's beloved St. Paul
repeatedly stated, to talk apparent folly. There is no
proof that God ever became man, though there is
some historical evidence that He did. The reader of
the New Testament may or may not accept the evidence. Augustine came to accept it, and by his acceptance made the great leap that he had despaired

of making. He made it by despairing of every alternative. He made it in tears and by an act of will: he chose Christ. Unless the reader understands the implications of the choice, he risks finding in the *Confessions* a magnificent psychological poem at best, and at worst, the triumph of fanaticism over bestiality.

Augustine's friend Alypius, like many men, came to believe in the incarnate Christ easily and gracefully. Augustine came the hard way. He desired passionately to escape from a slavery to sensual pleasure that he knew was destroying him and cutting him off from another sort of life. He had read Cicero's *Hortensius* in praise of what Socrates meant by philosophy: the love and pursuit of wisdom. He wanted to escape his bondage. But he could not will to, at least not enough to escape. He tried to will to will enough, and could not. His life therefore took on a horror familiar to anybody who has had a certain kind of nightmare, and perhaps to anybody who has struggled without success to escape from a driving physical appetite that is ruining his life.

In Plato's *Republic* the young, through music and gymnastic, and later through mathematics, are led to form moral habits that will allow them to pursue wisdom, which in turn will lead them to understand why those early habits were inculcated. But in the late Roman Empire, in the North African province of Numidia, Augustine had learned lust physically and eristic or sophistry intellectually. He had come to see through both lust and sophistry, but habit held him. When he turned to prayer, therefore, he prayed: "Give me chastity and continency, only not yet." [10] He was a grown man, a brilliant man, with the unbridled appetite of an adolescent. In his search for a more adult life he came eventually to Plato himself. But how would a man in his condition make the first start on the road that Socrates pointed out and that Augustine himself could recognize? He lived in what *The Republic,* in some of its darkest pages, describes as a tyrannical political state. But his own soul was what *The Republic* describes as the tyrannical soul. All through Roman society men and women were facing the same problem.

The student of Plato will recognize in Augustine's predicament a problem of form and matter. He will recognize in it, too, the connection between the intellectual virtues and the moral virtues, which Aristotle raises. Man, bound to the material universe about him by the very matter in his own body, can "see" things that are not material, and apparently only in those things can he find happiness. In the light of that invisible world he can apparently order the world of the senses, can find out what is true about it, what is good about it, and what is beautiful in it. But the senses constantly mislead him, constantly place a drag on his ability to "see."

When the tension between those two worlds became unbearable, Augustine, weeping and desperate, turned to Christ Incarnate, in whom spirit had become flesh. It was he, Augustine learned, who could alone mediate between the human and the divine, because he himself was both. In the four *Gospels* Augustine read the moving story of how God walked among men and died that they might live. In the *Acts of the Apostles* he read of those who

had believed on him. In the *Epistles* of St. Paul he
heard the words of a man who had made the "turn,"
the conversion, that he, Augustine, longed to make.
And he chose to follow. His "two wills," which had
tormented him by their discord, had become one.
Augustine might not as yet possess that vision of the
Good that Plato's guardians might win through to,
after long training in dialectic. He might not know
yet that brief but healing bliss that Aristotle believed the contemplative philosopher might possess.
But his voluntary subjection to the will of his chosen
Mediator guaranteed him, he believed, the hope of
that bliss to come, not briefly but eternally. Not by
first knowing the true in order to know and love
the good, would he come to his haven; but by loving first the Good Incarnate, which came down to
earth for his salvation, would he come to know whatever truth it would be his to know.

Where the Stoic had found self-restraint and acceptance of nature, Augustine found rapturous love
and overflowing joy. Where the Stoic asked little,
Augustine had demanded much and now found
more than he had demanded. He had demanded to
love the human world about him, but on all sides he
had seemed to see evil incarnate, evil that ensnared
him from the invisible world that Plato praised and
that he, Augustine, would fain see, too. Now he
loved all that truly existed, and above all God who
made the rest to exist. Socrates believed wistfully,
and without proof, that the soul would shuffle off its
mortality and find reward or punishment in the
invisible world to which it even now had partial
access. Lucretius believed that the world of visible

and tangible things was the only existent world and that death was the dissolution into component atoms, not only of the body but of the soul. Augustine had faith in the God-Man, Jesus of Nazareth, who suffered death upon the cross for our redemption from Lucretius' world; he had hope of knowing and loving God eternally; he had charity, love, for all things that truly are. And thus he added to the moral and intellectual virtues that Aristotle thought within our power to acquire, three others, the so-called theological virtues, pointed out by the Apostle Paul to the Corinthians, to Augustine, and to the world of men: faith, hope, and charity.

As for the blissful moment that Plato and Aristotle spoke of, that moment could be eternal, and Augustine talked of it with Monica, his mother, shortly after his conversion: ". . . she and I stood alone, leaning in a certain window, which looked into the garden of the house where we now lay, at Ostia; . . . We were discoursing then together, alone, . . . enquiring between ourselves in the presence of the Truth, which Thou art, of what sort the eternal life of the saints was to be, *which eye hath not seen, nor ear heard, nor hath it entered into the heart of man. . . .*[11]

"We were saying then: If to any the tumult of the flesh were hushed, hushed the images of earth, and waters, and air, hushed also the poles of heaven, yea the very soul be hushed to herself, and by not thinking on self surmount self, hushed all dreams and imaginary revelations, every tongue and every sign, and whatsoever exists only in transition, since if any could hear, all these say, *We made not ourselves, but*

He made us that abideth for ever— If then having uttered this, they too should be hushed, having roused only our ears to Him who made them, and He alone speak, not by them, but by Himself, that we may hear His Word, not through any tongue of flesh, nor Angel's voice, nor sound of thunder, nor in the dark riddle of a similitude, but, might hear Whom in these things we love, might hear His Very Self without these, (as we two now strained ourselves, and in swift thought touched on that Eternal Wisdom, which abideth over all;)—could this be continued on, and other visions of a kind far unlike be withdrawn, and this one ravish, and absorb, and wrap up its beholder amid these inward joys, so that life might be for ever like that one moment of understanding which now we sighed after; were not this, *Enter into thy Master's joy?* And when shall that be? When *we shall all rise again,* though we *shall not all be changed?*" [12]

This was the form of happiness that Augustine sought. For him, as for Aristotle, all men seek happiness. But for Augustine, the moral and intellectual virtues of Aristotle's *Ethics* are not enough to take most men even as far as Aristotle believed they would take a philosopher. Faith, hope, and charity must be added to the list. But with these added, man can know not merely moments of happiness but eternal happiness itself. It is towards this happiness, then, that all his acts must be ordered.

Among man's acts are his political and social acts, which also must conduce to this same final and eternal happiness, union with God his Creator. The consequences for political thinking are enormous.

What those consequences are Augustine was forced by events to clarify. In 410 A.D. the Visigoths captured Rome and sacked it. This catastrophe drove home to the imagination of men that they were witnessing that recurrent but always terrible phenomenon, the collapse of a whole civilization. In their agony they cried out that Rome had fallen because so many of her citizens had turned away from her gods to this strange, new, other-worldly, and hence uncivic doctrine of Christ the Savior—who had not saved Rome.

Augustine, Bishop of Hippo and citizen of Rome, was called upon to answer this grave charge. His answer was a Christian philosophy of history and politics, *The City of God*. In the first five books of this work he attacked the belief that devotion to Rome's pagan deities could have saved the Eternal City. In the next five he answers the claim that the traditional beliefs were at least a good preparation for the life to come. The remaining twelve books are devoted, to use his own description, to comparing the respective origins, histories, and destinies of the City of God and the City of the World. Between these two Cities is a great gulf fixed: how wide a gulf Augustine knew from direct experience, for he himself had crossed that gulf in agony of soul and then only by help of an Incarnate and Risen God, a God who had taken on human flesh precisely to help him cross. The fundamental and formidable choice before Everyman is the choice of whether or not to grasp the extended hand of that Mediator and to claim his waiting heritage of citizenship in the City of God.

It is man's glory that by nature he belongs in the City of God, the City of which Adam and Lucifer were alike citizens before each fell. It is man's misery that because Adam did fall, each of us is born outside that City, each of us is born a citizen of the City of the World, which Lucifer founded in rebellious pride. It is our misery that we seek to find happiness this side of the knowledge and love of our Creator, and it is our tragic glory that we inevitably fail.

To find intelligibility either in human history or in the science of human politics, Augustine had felt forced to turn back in time to a point before either human history or human politics existed, to a conflict among higher beings than men, beings then and now invisible. Human history becomes a reflection of this cosmic conflict, intelligible in its light and only in its light. It is perhaps this fact which gives his historical thought its Homeric majesty. Had not Homer, too, despaired of picturing the human conflict on the plains of Troy without relating to his listeners that even greater conflict which it reflected, the conflict between the gods on Mount Olympus? Do not Homer's gods intervene in the struggles of men as Satan intervened that day in Eden and still intervenes with Adam's breed? On this titanic canvas of gods—or angels—and men Augustine recapitulates the events of human history, drawing naturally from the center of that struggle the history of that people chosen especially by God, as related in the Old Testament.

Then comes what to Augustine is necessarily the key fact of all human history, the Intervention of interventions, the Incarnation: "the Son of God, *by taking up manhood without laying down his Godhead,* established and founded this faith so that to the God of man there might be a way for man through the God-man. For this is the mediator between God and man, the man Christ Jesus." [13] This mediation has furnished men a bridge across that vast chasm that separates Lucifer's City of the World from the City of God.

By crossing that bridge the individual man can find the means of ordering his life, his now inordinate desires, his now conflicting purposes. Eventually he can attain to that perfect happiness that Plato and Aristotle seemed to be, somewhat wistfully, talking about; and that Augustine and Monica, gazing from a window in Ostia, were certainly talking about: the contemplation and enjoyment of God. But in addition, he increases by one the citizenship of a Republic, a Republic unlike the pagan republic of the Romans, which after many Platonic vicissitudes, had finally fallen to the plundering Goth. Plato's Republic was, by Socrates' own statement, a pattern laid up in heaven, never yet duplicated among men. And yet whatever goodness the republics of men may achieve is the reflection of the perfect goodness of that invisible Republic.

But the Incarnate God has built a bridge that leads here and now to the City of God, a City partly inhabited by those angels who did not desert with Lucifer, partly by those saints and martyrs and others who died in Christ's faith, and partly by those living men who profess his name and who trust in his redeeming power. Thus a Christian Society comes into being, an earthly province as it were, of a greater society that includes the angelic host and those released from the bondage of this earth by death in the faith. True, this Christian Society coincides with the boundaries of no earthly political state nor is the political state its primary interest. But if enough men choose it, and choose it with enough intensity of faith, it could rebuild civilization and political order and even economic sufficiency along far nobler and more satisfying lines than those of a Rome the Goths had just destroyed. Meanwhile, this Christian Society, this City of God, is necessarily a "pilgrim city," moving through human history as the children of Israel moved through the desert towards a land that had been promised them and that would be home indeed. To the charge that the rise of Christianity had destroyed civilization, Augustine thus replies that only through Christianity can a worthy civilization be born or flourish. A good political state is possible on earth only to the extent that its citizens make it a province of the City of God. Human history interests Augustine. So does human government. But only because they are flickering shadows of a drama partly outside time and a government partly outside human politics.

Nearly eight and a half centuries of European history were unrolled between Augustine's Homeric picture of the City of God and the production by Thomas Aquinas of the *Summa Theologica*. The "pilgrim city of Christ the King" had made its pilgrimage through a civilization still predominantly pagan. By Thomas's day the pilgrim city had taken over Western Europe and had created another culture which, bloody and unChristlike as it was in many ways, was yet stamped unmistakably with Christian thought, with Christian imagery, with Christian institutions. Much of the new culture was built from the debris of the old, as Christian churches were built from stone which had been quarried from the ancient pagan monuments. Or indeed, as the Pantheon in Rome, dedicated to all the gods, was re-dedicated to One God and became a Christian church. It was indeed the same stone, but reset now to a different end. Doric temple gave way to Gothic cathedral, Greek or Roman column to flying buttress, graven images of the tired gods of Olympus to vigorous, if sometimes primitive, images of saints. And Aphrodite and Hera, their ancient quarrel buried now beneath the ruins of successive Troys, had both yielded to the Blessed Virgin, Mother of God.

Where Augustine, seeking aid in interpreting Holy Scripture, had turned to Plato, Thomas Aquinas turned to Aristotle. To Thomas, Aristotle was simply "the Philosopher," as Paul was simply "the Apostle." Indeed, Thomas had set himself a task not unlike the task that Aristotle had himself chosen: the ordering of all existing human knowledge in an intelligible system. And Aristotle and Thomas are among the few thinkers in recorded history who have seriously attempted that feat.

The contemporary reader is likely to be repelled by that attempt, and this for several excellent reasons. Accustomed as the contemporary reader is to a specialization that is proud of the fragmentary character of its investigation, Thomas's intellectual courage may strike him as temerity and arrogance. Accustomed as the contemporary reader is to equate knowledge with "scientific fact," Thomas may strike him as "abstract" and therefore vague and arid. Abstract the *Summa* most certainly is; but few writings have ever been less vague. Even if the contemporary reader has taken the precaution of reading Aristotle first, the tight, clear, Aristotelian terms of Thomas's analysis are likely to make him feel crowded, cornered, bullied. His defense will probably be that it is not all that simple, that it is much more complicated than that. It is indeed, as Thomas quite obviously knows. But how can the complicated, the particular, the accidental ever be fruitfully approached unless we first discern behind it and shining through it the simple, the general, the basic? How "come down to cases" unless we know what this is a case of? Above all, the contemporary reader will feel he has found the ideal case of medieval logic-chopping, scholastic verbalizing, and dogmatic assertion. A reasonably patient study of Thomas will dispel these high-school notions. Seldom have words been more successfully used to refer to something other than themselves. Seldom has a mind been more sweetly reasonable. Dogma there most certainly is: Thomas is interpreting the knowledge of his generation by the light of Christian dogmas, as well as by the light of philosophical principles that can be reached by natural reason. And Thomas understood perfectly a point of Aristotle's that has escaped most contemporary readers: that all demonstrative argument must eventually go back to propositions that are accepted without argument. For Thomas, as for Aristotle, some of these can be known intuitively; but to these Thomas, unlike Aristotle, adds those "revealed" by God to man. And it is these revealed truths that smell so mustily of the Sunday school to many a modern nostril and crown the modern's other objections to the *Summa Theologica*. But there can have been few modern Sunday schools that bear more than a most superficial verbal resemblance to the *Summa Theologica*.

Finally, the very name of Thomas Aquinas suggests Thomism, which suggests Neo-Thomism; and neo-anything is a repellant idea, like the idea of hash served a second time after it has been sent back to the kitchen once by common acclaim. Well, Karl Marx is said to have remarked once that he was not a Marxist, and certainly Thomas is no Neo-Thomist. The epithets of polemic have always proved notoriously incompetent guides to great reading.

For the present enquiry it is perhaps most worth noting that not even Plato or Aristotle makes it clearer that the ethical problem, the political problem, and the economic problem are soluble only in terms of the concept of the Good, of the concept of human happiness; hence ethics, science, and economics are "practical sciences," not "theoretical sciences"; they deal with ends and with the appropriate means to those ends. Economics deals with the production and distribution of material means to a good political state; and the political state must be judged good or bad as it provides adequate or inadequate means to the leading of a morally good life by its citizens; and the moral behavior of its citizens must be judged finally by whether it brings them closer to their proper final end, the knowledge and love of God through all eternity. As for Aristotle, therefore, so for Thomas, economic theory is subordinate to political theory, which is subordinate to ethical theory. But where ethics crowns Aristotle's practical enquiries (even though it depends intellectually on the purely theoretical science of metaphysics or, to use Aristotle's own term, *theologia*), theology crowns even the practical sciences for Thomas, as well as the theoretical.

Like the Aristotelian man, the Thomistic man must be prudent, courageous, temperate, and just. But in addition to these moral virtues and in addition to Aristotle's intellectual virtues, God may "infuse" in him by grace, gratuitously, as a free gift, the three theological virtues that Paul had named and that Augustine had already discussed: faith, hope, and charity. These three, the greatest of which is charity, are the only gates to the City of God.

The Great Divide remains the Incarnation of Jesus Christ. The "good news," the Gospel of that Incarnation, is, in terms of Thomas's universe, inconceivably good indeed. Before Christ came, a man who had the intellectual capacity for dialectic, and the time and opportunity to develop that capacity, might attain to fleeting if tantalizing glimpses of the Good itself, and those glimpses would be a happiness most men could never achieve. After Christ came, all men were invited to accept through the Church, the assembly of the faithful, the means of grace, of "saving grace." This "salvation" would be precisely from the City of the World, whose destiny is eternal damnation—the damnation of being cut off from God and hence from happiness. Salvation would be into the City of God, whose destiny is eternal bliss in the union with God. The bliss of seeing God face to face might occur briefly on this earth, though not necessarily to a great philosopher. More moderate happiness might be attained by many, as it had been before Christ came, through living a morally virtuous life. But if Monica and Augustine were right in their belief that "we shall all rise again," then what happens eternally after we rise will make what happens briefly or in moderate degree here and now seem tame.

If because Thomas shared that belief, the modern reader expects him to slur over the here and now or to think dishonestly about it, he will be surprised. On the moral and intellectual virtues, for example, Thomas is clearer, more orderly, and more incisive than "the Philosopher"—or at least than the surviving manuscripts ascribed to the Philosopher. There have been few more illuminating commentaries on Aristotle than the *Summa*. If Thomas attached more importance to the theological virtues than to the intellectual virtues, to God's power than to his own power, it is not because he lacked intellectual power himself. On the contrary, the *Summa* is one of the most brilliant examples of clear and penetrating analysis that human history affords. If the modern reader accepts the faith that Thomas held, Thomas can help him understand the implications of that faith. If he rejects it or is indifferent to it, he will do wisely to grant it for the sake of argument and see where it leads him. For it will most surely lead him to a great many insights into the most mundane and least "dogmatic" problems. The intelligent man, whether he be Christian, Jew, or agnostic, cannot afford to ignore the *Summa,* if only because it says clearly too many things that he himself is likely to be saying fuzzily.

The beauty of Thomas Aquinas, like the beauty of Aristotle, is the cool beauty of clarity and precision. Their ideas do not trail behind them the glorious and moving imagery of a Plato or an Augustine. For images that will worthily show forth the beauty of Thomas's universe, one should turn to the majestic poem of a poet who studied him faithfully; one should turn to *The Divine Comedy* of Dante Alighieri. Thomas analyzed the Christian universe and showed the proper relation of its parts. Dante saw that universe with his own eyes—all of it, including hell, purgatory, and heaven itself—loved all of it, even in a very genuine sense, hell; and made it live in the imagination of man. Dante is perhaps the only poet who ever went clear to hell to get a poem. He got a good one, maybe because he went to heaven, too, before he wrote it. The poem is an epic and he himself is its hero, and in going to hell he is acting in the great tradition. Odysseus had gone to hell, and had to, or not make port. In Virgil's great epic, Æneas went there, and had to, if he would found Eternal Rome. Perhaps it is appropriate then, that in *The Divine Comedy,* it is Virgil who escorts Dante there, and to purgatory, too, and instructs him in what he observes. Thomas had dissected an entire universe; only a hero poet, one willing to go through hell with Virgil, could have made these bones live again. Perhaps if Dante had tackled fewer parts than make up a universe, he would have failed. But his daring drove him to tackle all of it; and the integrity of Thomas's philosophic subject-matter becomes the integrity of Dante's poetic subject-matter. He is meticulous about points of Thomistic doctrine, as he is meticulous about points in Ptolemaic astronomy, and yet he is not pedantic. He is the final living proof that a poet cannot be too philosophical, or too scientific, to write a poem.

Not only does love of abstract truth never block his imaginative grasp of beauty. That grasp is never weakened by his moral fervor. He wrote his friend and patron, Can Grande: that . . . "the end of the whole [*The Divine Comedy*] and of the part [*The Paradise*] is to remove those living in this life from the state of misery and lead them to the state of felicity.

"But the *branch of philosophy* which regulates the work in its whole and in its parts, is morals or ethics, because the whole was undertaken not for speculation but for practical results." [14] Dante is the final living proof that a poet cannot be too concerned with right and wrong to write a good poem.

Despite the musical grace of the new Italian tongue in which Dante wrote, and which by choosing to write in it, he largely prepared to be the language of a national state, the total effect of the poem is antique Roman, monumental, sculptural. Again, does not this quality derive from his glad acceptance of great and firm philosophic principles? Is he not history's most convincing witness that the principles of Thomas's philosophy spell freedom, not confinement, to him who takes the pains to grasp them?

Dante's daring in confronting as a poet the hell that Thomas had treated as a philosopher was richly rewarded. This embittered political exile from Florence found all his worst enemies there, at least those who had already departed this life. Those who had placed him in exile Dante placed in hell. He found there also the popes and other supporters of papal power and glory who had corrupted and debauched the Church of Christ and by their ecclesiastical maneuvers for political advantage kept Dante's beloved Italy a cockpit. Even in the case of enemies who were still alive and who enjoyed, so to speak, an alibi, Dante was able to report from nethermost hell that its incumbents predicted their imminent arrival. No poet has ever improved on this method of publicly disgracing his recently deceased enemies: to report a personal journey to hell and to include a vivid picture of the actual torments the poet's enemies are currently undergoing.

But this grim satisfaction is followed, when Dante ascends through Ptolemy's successive spheres to paradise, by the joy of conversing with the great saints of the Church. And it is crowned by the final ecstasy that Plato and Aristotle spoke of darkly and that Augustine and Thomas hailed with joy and Christian confidence: the beatific vision when man looks on the face of God. This ecstasy Dante achieved at the end of his mystic journey, and it is the culmination of his poem.

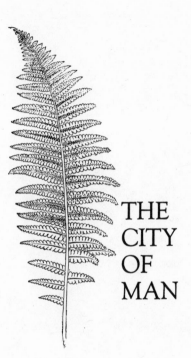

THE
CITY
OF
MAN

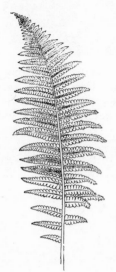

THE
CITY
OF
MAN

The number of prominent citizens, including ecclesiastics, whom Dante met in hell, boded ill for the "pilgrim city."

By the time Machiavelli and Hobbes wrote, that city was indeed in bad shape. Both *The Prince* and the *Leviathan* are shrewd, skeptical handbooks for practical politicians, heads of Italian city-states or of the new national kingdoms in Western Europe, more interested in political survival than in theological salvation.

Machiavelli preferred republics to tyrannies, and democratic republics to aristocratic ones. But in *The Prince* he is not concerned to air his preferences, but to set forth objectively the ways by which autocratic rulers seek and secure power. He therefore exemplifies the modern conception of political science as an autonomous study. He not only dumps as irrelevant to his purpose the theological premises on which Augustine and Thomas built their political theories; he dumps the ethical premises which they took over from Plato and Aristotle. He is interested not in what the state ought to be in theory but

83 ❧

in what states appear to be in fact. He therefore advises aspiring princes to lie, cheat, steal, murder—and pretend to be models of Christian virtue. For, he ironically observes, these methods seem to work in power politics where the Christian virtues lead only to ruin. It is not surprising that his candor has scandalized every succeeding generation or that, on the whole, they have found his advice apparently useful. The candid reader, who will apply his maxims to the contemporary political scene, will be overwhelmed by the sharp light they throw on events. Machiavelli is as concerned with ends and means as Plato or Thomas is, but in *The Prince* he assumes as the ruler's final end the material power of the state. Whether this is a good end he leaves an open question; and by leaving it open, he infuses an almost Socratic irony into his writing that will even enable *The Prince* to be read as a lampoon against tyrants. His book is short, hard, cold, and brilliant.

Where Machiavelli observes ironically that rulers who ignore morality appear to win all the prizes, Hobbes attempts to define philosophically the position of the ruler as being above criticism. He does not propose to base his philosophy of the state upon Platonic considerations of a Dialectical Republic: ". . . I am at the point of believing this my labour, as uselesse, as the Commonwealth of *Plato;* For he also is of opinion that it is impossible for the disorders of State, and change of Governments by Civill Warre, ever to be taken away, till Soveraigns be Philosophers. But when I consider again, that the Science of Naturall Justice, is the onely Science necessary for Soveraigns, and their principall Ministers;

and that they need not be charged with the Sciences Mathematicall, (as by *Plato* they are,) further, than by good Lawes to encourage men to the study of them; and that neither *Plato,* nor any other Philosopher hitherto, hath put into order, and sufficiently or probably proved all the Theoremes of Morall doctrine, that men may learn thereby, both how to govern, and how to obey; I recover some hope, that one time or other, this writing of mine, may fall into the hands of a Soveraign, who will consider it himselfe, (for it is short, and I think clear,) without the help of any interested, or envious Interpreter; and by the exercise of entire Soveraignty, in protecting the Publique teaching of it, convert this Truth of Speculation, into the Utility of Practice." [15]

Neither the final aim of man, nor his highest good, in the theological sense, seems relevant to Hobbes: ". . . the Felicity of this life, consisteth not in the repose of a mind satisfied. For there is no such *Finis ultimus,* (utmost ayme,) nor *Summum Bonum,* (greatest Good,) as is spoken of in the Books of the old Morall Philosophers." [16] Nor will Hobbes tolerate Scholastic talk of beatific visions, of seeing God's face even in this life, nor even speak of just what joys await us in paradise: "What kind of Felicity God hath ordained to them that devoutly honour him, a man shall no socner know, than enjoy; being joyes, that now are as incomprehensible, as the word of Schoole-men *Beatificall Vision* is unintelligible." [17]

Hobbes is enough in the scholastic tradition to furnish the reader with a treatise on the nature of man before trying to discover the conditions under which he can be politically controlled. Man, as Hobbes pictures him, is very like other animals except for his dangerously competitive desire for power, his capacity for speech, and his insatiable curiosity. This last Hobbes calls "a Lust of the mind, that by a perseverance of delight in the continuall and indefatigable generation of Knowledge, exceedeth the short vehemence of any carnall Pleasure." [18]

This dangerous and somewhat mechanical animal has no free will, which greatly simplifies Hobbes' problem of finding the correct rule for governing him politically, ". . . which Rules neither poor men have the leisure, nor men that have had the leisure, have hitherto had the curiosity, or the method to find out." [19] It is obvious by now that Hobbes will make political science a supreme science. It will rebel against both ethics and theology; it will just as surely hold economics in subjection. The king holds his authority direct from God, including the authority to instruct the people in ethics and theology as in all other matters. A bishop would have to hold his from the king. The "Kingdome of God" is not the Church, certainly not the Roman Catholic Church with its long history of contesting for political power. The Kingdome of God is not in this world at all but in the next. This world is ruled by "Soveraigns." The papacy's efforts to usurp political authority make it "the Kingdome of Darknesse" and reflect the fact that it "is no other, than the *Ghost* of the deceased *Romane Empire,* sitting crowned upon the grave thereof: for so did the Papacy start up on a Sudden out of the Ruines of that Heathen

Power." [20] In this modern, all-powerful state, this monster Leviathan, there will naturally be no talk of economic rights or of laws transcending those of the political order. All property rights derive from the sovereign, since without political order private ownership disappears in anarchy and chaos. All economic corporations are creatures of the sovereign and must bow to his will. "Inexorable laws" will be located not in economics but in political science.

There will be no "right of revolution." The problem Sophocles raised in his *Antigone* will disappear. There can be no unjust law, because it is the law that defines justice, at least on this earth. No tyrannicide can be defended, because tyrant is merely the name subjects give a monarch they dislike. The one escape from Leviathan is the one Socrates chose: we are "free" to die if we do not like the necessary political condition of man on this earth. This is the view of the state that seemed best to accord with Hobbes' experience, an experience that included the religious wars that tore Christendom to shreds and, in England, a political revolution that cost a king his head. Hobbes is trying to find an escape from violence and anarchy, the same kind of political and moral anarchy that Thucydides shows us raging at Corcyra and spreading like an evil cancer through the Hellenic world.

Hobbes hopes to find the escape from anarchy in principles of government as sure as those in his beloved mathematics, a field in which he thought himself abler than he actually was. He feared, in considering his problem, to be tricked like the others by metaphor; and he was one of the greatest masters of metaphor who ever wrote. He loathed Aristotle and eschewed him in favor of his own clear reason; and his argument contains openings that Aristotle would have been quick to exploit. Unlike Machiavelli, he insisted on discussing ethics and theology; and the discussion is the least good part of his work.

But the eloquence of Hobbes in speaking of the actual operation of power politics is based on genuine and deep perception. A human community cannot live tolerably without government and law. "Hereby it is manifest, that during the time men live without a common Power to keep them all in awe, they are in that condition which is called warre; and such a warre, as is of every man, against every man. For WARRE, consisteth not in Battell onely, or the act of fighting; but in a tract of time, wherein the Will to contend by Battell is sufficiently known: and therefore the notion of *Time,* is to be considered in the nature of Warre; as it is in the nature of Weather. For as the nature of Foule weather, lyeth not in a showre or two of rain; but in an inclination thereto of many dayes together: So the nature of War, consisteth not in actuall fighting; but in the known disposition thereto, during all the time there is no assurance to the contrary. All other time is PEACE.

"Whatsoever therefore is consequent to a time of Warre, where every man is Enemy to every man; the same is consequent to the time, wherein men live without other security, than what their own strength, and their own invention shall furnish them withall. In such condition, there is no place for Industry; be-

cause the fruit thereof is uncertain: and consequently no Culture of the Earth; no Navigation, nor
use of the commodities that may be imported by Sea;
no commodious Building; no Instruments of moving, and removing such things as require much
force; no Knowledge of the face of the Earth; no
account of Time; no Arts; no Letters; no Society;
and which is worst of all, continuall feare, and danger of violent death; And the life of man, solitary,
poore, nasty, brutish, and short." [21]

Does the reader suppose there never has existed
such a period of total anarchy? Hobbes answers that
he is not talking about an epoch in time but about
a limiting condition, and a limit rapidly approached
in civil war or whenever government and law falter.
Moreover, we can judge this limiting condition, this
state of nature in which every man's hand is against
every man, by the curious relation that still subsists
between sovereigns. We of the twentieth century
have been calling this relation white war, gray war,
cold war, and such terms. To Hobbes it is plain
"Warre," whether the shooting is going on at the
time or not. For there is no government, no law,
higher than sovereign states to keep the peace. Their
relation is therefore an essentially anarchical relation, and they face each other (and indeed must face
each other) "in the state and posture of Gladiators;
having their weapons pointing, and their eyes fixed
on one another; that is, their Forts, Garrisons, and
Guns upon the Frontiers of their Kingdomes; and
continuall Spyes upon their neighbours; which is a
posture of War." [22]

To secure a modicum of peace at least in one area,

to secure themselves against "the invasion of For-raigners, and the injuries of one another," [23] men covenant together to obey one man or one assembly of men—in short, one sovereign. Thus united in one "person" or representative, authorized to act for all of them, a "Common-wealth" is generated. "This is the Generation of that great LEVIATHAN, or rather (to speake more reverently) of that *Mortall God,* to which wee owe under the *Immortall God,* our peace and defense." [24] This Mortal God, whom Hobbes so much reveres, can be deliberately set up, as was done by the Americans at Philadelphia, or tacitly sub-mitted to, following conquest. In any case, it is all that Hobbes believes can save civilization.

Machiavelli and Hobbes are both, of course, deeply heretical, in terms of the intellectual tradi-tion and in the original etymological sense of the word heresy. For they have "chosen out" certain im-portant propositions from Europe's political think-ing and denied their subordination to other propo-sitions. But like many heresies, theirs are illuminat-ing and worth understanding. By dropping the bur-den of ethical, let alone theological, considerations they have increased their energy in dealing with the political problem in isolation and out of context. And although this loss of context may have falsified and vitiated their thinking, almost any page of either *The Prince* or the *Leviathan* seems cruelly apposite today. To shift the metaphor, by focusing their philosophic lens sharply on politics, they have dis-torted our view of the moral premises of political action; but once you have looked at what they bring

in focus, you will not forget it. For soft-headed thinking both books are specifics.

We can measure the distortion by comparing
Thomistic man with Hobbesean man. Thomistic
man is corrupt as the result of original sin, the sin
of pride in Adam, and this cuts him off from the salvation that is his only true happiness. Hobbesean
man is corrupt as the result of his lust for power,
and this cuts him off from political order which is
his true happiness. Thomistic man is redeemed from
original sin by the mediation of Jesus Christ; but
Hobbesean man is redeemed from political anarchy
and physical violence by his desire for security and
by the use of his reason to covenant with his fellows
and achieve it. Thomistic man, in a state of grace,
submits joyfully to the will of God. Hobbesean man,
in a state of political order, submits intelligently to
the will of the sovereign. One achieves citizenship
in the City of God; the other becomes the subject of
a political state. Thomistic man's highest aim is salvation; and Hobbesean man's highest aim is physical
self-preservation. For Thomas, political science is a
department of applied theology; for Hobbes, theology is a department of government—or what we
moderns would call an ideology. That Hobbes accepts Christianity, at least as he interprets Scripture,
changes no item in this list. On this earth, Leviathan,
a "Mortall God," has the last word.

If Dante saw and painted the City of God which
Thomas had analyzed, then William Shakespeare
saw and painted the City of Man, ruled over by
Machiavellian princes and Hobbesean sovereigns.

Among all the resplendent dramas of Shakespeare, not one revolves centrally around the religious theme that was Dante's basic illumination. Shakespeare is concerned with a new kind of man, with him who inhabits the City of Man, proud, ambitious, confident, exulting in his human powers. Even in his misery Hamlet could cry: "What a piece of work is a man! how noble is reason! how infinite in faculties! in form and moving, how express and admirable! in action, how like an angel! in apprehension, how like a god! the beauty of the world! the paragon of animals!" [25]

Man's glory lies no longer in his dependence on God but on what he can achieve unaided, by his infinite faculties and by his noble reason. There are indeed still angels, but how much like them man acts! He is godlike, he is—an animal with all but perfect powers. Francis Bacon would tell him how easily he could subject all nature to his glorying will and seize material power he had as yet not dreamed of, if he would but focus his reason continuously and systematically on studying Nature's laws, if he would "obey" Nature in order to cunningly master her. Then would the City of Man become a land of milk and honey indeed. Better: by systematically studying Nature he could "in some part" recapture Eden, where by his fall he had lost "his dominion over creation." Yet Shakespeare knew more than man's new-found glory: he knew man's misery, too. He knew how often human existence appeared to be only "a tale told by an idiot, full of sound and fury, signifying nothing."

If man be godlike by virtue of his power of reason, and through reason his power over the rest of creation, then surely the most godlike man, because the most powerful, would be the prince, the sovereign. This, surely, and not some cheap snobbery, must be why Shakespeare shows us a pageant of so many kings: Prince Harry trying on his father's crown, then as King Henry V soliloquizing on the eve of battle upon the heaviness of that crown; the murderous Richard III; the great Caesar stricken down for reaching after more than crowns; Macbeth selling his soul to occult powers to hold a scepter; old Lear trying to divide a crown, trying also to preserve some of the emoluments of kingship without the heavy burden, learning like Odysseus what sovereignty is like by beggary and exile. For one of the themes that most haunted Shakespeare's mind was that of the prince, the sovereign, that half-mystical being who plays in the City of Man the role reserved in the City of God to God alone.

With the City of God fading slowly from man's view and with the brave new City of Man looming larger and more brilliant each day, a strange thing happened. A gentle, quiet, resigned Amsterdam Jew named Spinoza, with incredible intellectual daring, tried to put the two Cities together in a treatise on ethics, cast in the literary form of a treatise on geometry with definitions, axioms, postulates, propositions, corollaries, and even "Q.E.D."! It is a form that Aristotle never would have chosen, for a reason given in his own *Ethics:* that ethics cannot be as exact a science as mathematics. But despite this handicap, Spinoza's treatise is a book of great power.

Spinoza earned excommunication from the synagogue and denunciation from Christians by holding that God had a body—which was quite simply all the matter in the universe—as well as a mind. The body of any given man is part of God's body and his mind is a part of God's mind. A strict causation governs both mind and body. Freedom of the will is an illusion. We cannot, therefore, take the blind leap that Augustine took or thought he took. We are reminded of Plato's statement: that no man wittingly chooses evil. We simply desire whatever we understand to be "good"—that is, good for us, tending to preserve us. And we reject whatever we see will harm or destroy us, as being "evil." The prime desire of our mind is to understand, which is an end in itself. Emotion occurs when we understand only confusedly. Our task is to clarify our emotions and thereby enhance our understanding. The reason we think the will is "free" is that we are conscious of certain acts of ours without understanding what caused them. The moment we understand what caused them, we know they were necessary, were inexorably caused. Finally, since events outside us are also inexorably caused, happiness consists in understanding this fact and in accepting events equably as they occur.

Now this last advice is likely to remind us of the Stoics and their determination not to fret about things that were not within their power. But the Stoic was essentially unspeculative and, at his worst, moralizing. Spinoza values good moral acts only as means to intellectual insight. Man's highest happiness lies in the intuitive knowledge of God, in perfecting what Aristotle would have called the intellectual virtues until the intellect can behold the Good. "It is therefore extremely useful in life," says Spinoza, "to perfect as much as we can the intellect or reason, and of this alone does the happiness or blessedness of man consist: for blessedness (*beatitudo*) is nothing else than satisfaction of mind which arises from the intuitive knowledge of God." [26] This is as near to Thomas's beatific vision as Spinoza will come, and also as near to freedom as he will come. For a man's intuitive knowledge of God brings him "mental liberty or blessedness." Nor does Spinoza seek for Thomas's "eternal bliss" in a next life; he does not expect immortality in the Jewish or Christian sense; the mind achieves immortality only by escaping from time to eternity, as in contemplating God, for example. Rewards and punishments of the sort that Dante witnessed in hell and in heaven are therefore fictions. We do not by an act of will live righteously in order in the next life to see God. We understand here and now in order to know God; and if we know God, we will inevitably and necessarily live righteously.

Only the human intellect can restrain human lusts; there is no miraculous "grace," no incarnation of the God-man, to do it for us. Then it may not be done at all? Then it will not be done, and happiness, "blessedness," will be missed—as, indeed, it usually is. Spinoza's *Ethics* ends with Proposition XLII: "Blessedness is not the reward of virtue, but virtue itself: nor should we rejoice in it for that we restrain our lusts, but, on the contrary, because we rejoice therein we can restrain our lusts." [27] There follows

the usual Proof, with citations of earlier Propositions and Proofs. Then a "note" with which the
Treatise ends:

"Thus I have completed all I wished to show concerning the power of the mind over emotions or the
freedom of the mind. From which it is clear how
much a wise man is in front of and how stronger he
is than an ignorant one, who is guided by lust alone.
For an ignorant man, besides being agitated in many
ways by external causes, never enjoys one true satisfaction of the mind: he lives, moreover, almost unconscious of himself, God, and things, and as soon as
he ceases to be passive, ceases to be. On the contrary,
the wise man, in so far as he is considered as such,
is scarcely moved in spirit: he is conscious of himself, of God, and things by a certain eternal necessity, he never ceases to be, and always enjoys satisfaction of mind. If the road I have shown to lead to
this is very difficult, it can yet be discovered. And
clearly it must be very hard when it is so seldom
found. For how could it be that it is neglected prac-
tically by all, if salvation were close at hand and
could be found without difficulty? But all excellent
things are as difficult as they are rare." [28]

Lest the reader think he detects intellectual snobbery in this passage, it should perhaps be added
that Spinoza gently suggests some very commonplace and very common-sense methods by which
those of us who are still "ignorant" may become wise.
These may be reduced to the advice to make simple
rules of conduct for ourselves and to form powerful
images of ourselves of wise responses to the chal-
lenges our lives habitually offer us, so that these

images may guide us until our ideas become clear enough to give us true guidance. This, after all, is the thing that Plato wanted "music" to do for the young in his republic; and Spinoza is essentially advising persons who are immature intellectually what kind of behavior will permit them to mature. For maturity, in this sense, is itself blessedness. It is a maturity which, despite a theology rejected by Jew and Christian alike, Spinoza makes the goal of a singularly "Christian" morality, a morality that instructs us even to return love for hatred.

This view of man and his moral problem leaves the monster Leviathan intact as the necessary means of controlling the ignorant, and therefore evil and turbulent, inhabitants of the City of Man in which we indubitably find ourselves; and then gently directs us to find the City of God, not in "the next life" but in this one, not by turning to a God-man (unless we are all God-men, our bodies parts of God's infinitely extended body, our minds modes of his eternal mind), but by turning inward to our hearts and minds. It is there and nowhere else that human happiness, "blessedness," a kind of beatific vision in so far as such a thing exists, may be safely sought and surely found.

To accept Leviathan is just what John Locke will not do. His *Two Treatises on Civil Government* were occasioned, it is true, not by Hobbes's *Leviathan,* but by the now half-forgotten writings of Sir Robert Filmer who had defended the divine right of kings. But Filmer's views were profoundly Hobbesian, and it was therefore in effect against the

Mortall God that Locke launched his first treatise, denouncing "certain false principles." It is in the second treatise that he rebuilds the City of Man nearer to the heart's desire. Augustine had attempted to give the origins, histories, and destinies of the Two Cities. Locke attempts to furnish the origin, the extent, and the end of civil government.

Locke deduces his theory of the political state, as Hobbes does, not from Christian theology or even from a system of ethics, but from "the state of nature"—the state in which man lived before government and law existed, or perhaps the state in which he would have to live if government and law ceased. But Locke's picture of the state of Nature differs radically from that of Hobbes. For Hobbes, man is naturally cunning, envious, and violent; and the state of Nature is therefore a hideous scene of violence, lust, discord, privation, fear, and animality. "And the life of man, solitary, poore, nasty, brutish, and short." [29] For Locke, man is naturally a reasonable and well-intentioned fellow; and "The state of Nature has a law of Nature to govern it, which obliges every one; and reason, which is that law, teaches all mankind who will but consult it, that, being all equal and independent, no one ought to harm another in his life, health, liberty, or possessions. . . ." [30] It teaches them also that every man in a state of Nature has a right to enforce this respect. Like Hobbes, Locke notes that all princes, or sovereigns, are still in this state with respect to each other: in international affairs each government has to take the law into its own hands in dealing with other governments, since each government is a sovereign. Still, it is law—the law of Nature, which is reason. Hobbes finds no moral law in the state of Nature—only the law of the jungle, which the other animals live by. It is only by setting up a state that moral law is brought into being. To set up such a state men, fearing each man his neighbor, covenant together to set up a despot, whether king or assembly, and agree to obey that despot. By placing themselves at the mercy of a sovereign, they escape from living at each other's mercy. But the covenant was made between themselves, not with the sovereign. Once they become his subjects, they can have no "rights" against the sovereign. Only absolute obedience to his will gives them whatever rights they do possess. His is the power of life and death.

This strikes Locke as absurd. It makes no sense to try to save your life—and your liberty and property, he would insist on adding—from a possibly violent neighbor by turning them all over without strings to a possibly violent sovereign. If your purpose in entering a political state is to guarantee by law that your relations with other men shall be relations of reason and not relations of force, why invite a relation of force with the one person or group of persons—the sovereign—who by definition is most able to take advantage of the situation? It appears to Locke that Hobbes' sovereign is not only in a state of war with all other sovereigns but is in a state of war with his own subjects as well. Finally, he appeals to an ancient theological point, and one that is both Socratic and Christian: a man has no right to take his own life, since his life belongs to God. It follows, says Locke, that he has no right to enslave himself either, by giving another the power to take his life at will.

Locke therefore holds that man in a state of Nature voluntarily forms with his neighbors a political community, and this community sets up a government and cedes to it, but only conditionally, the right and duty of enforcing law. Its function is to make and enforce laws, to regulate and preserve property, to protect its citizens against foreign agression—and "all this only for the public good." [31] If it fails to discharge those functions, it forfeits the powers of government and "the people" reassume the rights that belonged to them in the state of Nature, rights that cannot be permanently alienated in any event. The government is merely the instrument of those who deputized it in the first instance. Ultimate sovereignty resides in the "political community," not in the government it sets up, or submits to, conditionally. The community is provisionally responsible to the government, so long as it discharges its proper function. But finally, it is the other way around: government is responsible to the people. And who shall judge whether government discharges its proper function? "The people shall be judge," answers Locke, "for who shall be judge whether his trustee or deputy acts well and according to the trust reposed in him, but he who deputes him . . . ?" [32]

Because we dwellers in English-speaking lands have lived so long now in the tradition of John Locke, these words of his have lost some of their ring. But they were revolutionary words when uttered. They were intended to justify, among other things, the "Glorious Revolution" of 1688 that had dethroned James II and set William of Orange on the throne; and a century later they would be used to justify the American Revolution against George III.

But the words of Locke imply more than those two revolutions and more perhaps than Locke himself knew. For Locke holds that all men are born equal, and explains that their equality consists in their equal right to freedom under law, the political equivalent of the equal right of self-preservation that they would have in a state of Nature, had no government been set up to do the preserving for them. Apparently government is responsible to all the men it governs and to all the children, too, as fast as they grow up and attain to the full use of their reason. Yet the Glorious Revolution was the revolution of a small propertied class against their king; and the American Revolution would be essentially the revolution of a similar group. Did the rest of "the people" merely assent?

More significant still: all men are equal because all have an equal right to their "natural freedom," and this natural freedom includes not only their lives but their property. For the moral right to one's property exists independently of the state: it is a natural right, like freedom. No state can arbitrarily confiscate a man's property any more than it can arbitrarily confiscate a man's life or his liberty. For the origin of property is human labor. Even Hobbesian man, who cedes all property rights to the "Sovereign" and is glad if he comes out of his "covenant" with at least a whole skin, knows this much: that in order for a given parcel of the "matter" in the world about us to satisfy our basic physical wants, we often have to spend labor. We eat our bread by the sweat of our face, or of somebody else's face. "As for the Plenty of Matter," says Hobbes, "it is a thing limited by Nature, to those commodities, which from (the two breasts of our common Mother) Land, and Sea, God usually either freely giveth, or for labour selleth to man-kind." [33]

What every man purchases with his labor in this fashion, Locke holds, he has rightfully appropriated, and common to all though it may once have been, it is now his property. "Whatsoever, then, he removes out of the state that Nature hath provided and left it in, he hath mixed his labour with it, and joined to it something that is his own, and thereby makes it his property." [34] Nobody else has a right to what John Locke has mixed his labor with, "at least," adds Locke a little hesitantly, "where there is enough, and as good left in common for others." [35]

Thus, by Nature each of us possesses the right of self-preservation, of self-defense. Each of us possesses freedom to do whatever seems good to him, provided he does not destroy the freedom which his natural reason tells him his neighbor equally possesses. Each of us possesses equal rights to use the common resources of Nature, "the great common of the world," and to appropriate parcels of it by mixing our personal labor with it. To the extent that each of us works diligently and intelligently, each of us will then possess private property—provided, perhaps, there is still plenty for others to mix some labor with and to make private property out of. Government succeeds this idyllic state of Nature when we agree together to depute to chosen persons the job of defending the life of each of us, the liberty of each of us, and the private property of each of us.

So important to Locke is this right to one's private property, which Nature sells a man for his sweat, or perhaps once sold his father for that father's sweat, that he even uses the word "property" to describe all three of the basic natural rights that are proper to man. The dangers and inconveniences of the state of Nature lead men "to unite for the mutual preservation of their lives, liberties and estates, which I call by the general name—property.

"The great and chief end, therefore, of men uniting into commonwealths, and putting themselves under government, is the preservation of their property . . ." [36]

There is no natural limit, Locke holds, to how much private property a man may justly possess, unless it is in the form of perishable goods that would go to waste. "And thus came in the use of money; some lasting thing that men might keep without spoiling, and that, by mutual consent, men would take in exchange for the truly useful but perishable supports of life.

"And as different degrees of industry were apt to give men possessions in different proportions, so this invention of money gave them the opportunity to continue and enlarge them." [37]

Thus Locke is satisfied that he has justified private property as natural and not subject to expropriation by government, unless in the case of lawfully voted taxes; and has also justified as natural the vast inequality of private fortunes held by naturally equal citizens. Both of these two property rights are maintained by most "free" governments today; and the arguments advanced in defense of them remain basically Locke's arguments. Together they constitute what is often called the sanctity of private property.

One other vitally important power, which may also be properly termed natural, Locke holds to be the right and duty of regulating relations with persons or governments outside the commonwealth. For Locke agrees with Hobbes that any given commonwealth is necessarily in a state of Nature in relation to any other commonwealth. To Hobbes that means in a state of War, whether hostilities are being carried on by arms or by diplomacy. To Locke, with his more optimistic view of the state of Nature, it means that "the power of war and peace, leagues and alliances, and all the transactions with all persons and communities without the commonwealth" must belong to government "and may be called federative if any one pleases. So the thing be understood, I am indifferent as to the name." [38]

It is, of course, not the name commonly used today: the name today is sovereignty. But it is worth observing that it is a force relation, and a relation which Locke rejects flatly as between citizen and citizen or as between citizen and ruler. Those two relations he has converted from force relations, dependent provisionally on an appeal to reason but ultimately on an appeal to God, into lawful relations, precisely by setting up "civil government." It is only when government breaks down that citizen and citizen must appeal to reason, and if that breaks down, to God, to help the right side win by force. For society has then relapsed from a civil state to a state of Nature, to that anarchy which terrified Hobbes and disturbed even the serene and urbane expositor of "civil government." It is only when Government tyrannizes that the citizen has the natural right to appeal to reason, and if that breaks down, to God, to help him put down tyranny by force. For a tyrant by being tyrant has chosen to place himself in a state of Nature in relation to those over whom he tyrannizes.

But Locke admits, with less horror and indignation than Hobbes, that every sovereign state is in a state of Nature with respect to every other sovereign state. He knows therefore that there can be no appeal to law, but only an appeal to reason; and if that should fail, then to God, to help the right side impose its will by force. Locke must know, since it is implicit in his whole argument, what Hobbes saw more vividly: that sovereign states necessarily face each other "in the state and posture of Gladiators; having their weapons pointing, and their eyes fixed on one another; that is, their Forts, Garrisons, and Guns upon the Frontiers of their Kingdomes; and continuall Spyes upon their neighbours; which is a posture of War." [39]

It is natural, says Locke in effect, and therefore right that men should be politically free and equal. It is natural and therefore right that men should be economically free and unequal; though perhaps only if opportunity still exists for the poor to catch up with the rich and thereby achieve economic equality. It is natural and therefore right that relations between foreign states should know no law except the law of Nature, which is reason—a law clearly not good enough to guarantee either freedom or equality inside each state, a law that always tends to collapse into Hobbesian violence.

Locke's City of Man therefore is governed, not by the vision of the Good as beheld by the Platonic guardians of the Dialectical Republic, nor by the purpose of man's final reunion with a Thomistic God. Locke's City is not governed by anybody's knowledge, but by all men's opinions. For Locke is the great respecter of opinion, as distinguished from what your Platonic guardian or your Christian theologian may claim is more than opinion. The ideas the guardians saw with the mind's eye seemed to Plato more certain and therefore a more common social bond than did any sense perceptions, whether the artisans' or their own. The things men knew by either reason or revelation seemed to Thomas more secure than those they learned through their senses. Even Spinoza is looking for certainty and necessity, not in opinion or in the world of sense and emotion, but in the mind: it is easier to get agreement on geometry than on the things in the market-place. Let Hobbes's sovereign therefore rule by force the wrangling market-place, but let each of his subjects pass through geometrical certainty to the intuitive knowledge of God. But Locke objects. He agrees that the market-place wrangles; that is why an umpire called government, not a sovereign called a

Mortall God, must be appointed, subject to the majority opinion of the wranglers. This will at least prevent wrangling from degenerating into violence.

Locke's *Essay on Human Understanding* will not go as far towards scepticism as Hume's *An Enquiry Concerning Human Understanding*. But it will emphasize the experience of the senses as against the ideas in which both Plato's guardians and Thomas Aquinas placed their trust, and to that extent it justifies philosophically Locke's strong insistence on freedom, including freedom of opinion. Where the guardians would exercise a severe censorship in the interest of the truth they had beheld with the mind's eye; where Thomas would have burned the heretic who taught false doctrine; where Hobbes would give the government all power to teach those doctrines proper to the state; Locke stood staunchly for freedom of opinion, even in the still crucial matter of religion.

In *A Letter Concerning Toleration* Locke, therefore, indignantly denounced religious persecution, persecution for no matter what professedly high purpose: "For it will be very difficult to persuade men of sense that he who with dry eyes and satisfaction of mind can deliver his brother to the executioner to be burnt alive, does sincerely and heartily concern himself to save that brother from the flames of hell in the world to come." [40] He does not demand toleration of Roman Catholics, but only because he regards them as subjects of a foreign prince, the Pope. To say that the Pope ruled his considerable temporal dominions as prince, while he ruled his Church only as spiritual head, would never satisfy

Locke, since the two rulers were the same person. What fatal confusions he expects of such combinations of powers is apparent from his insistence on the separation of powers in a given civil government —the power to make laws, the power to enforce them, the power to judge who has broken them. He does not demand toleration for atheists because "Promises, covenants, and oaths, which are the bonds of human society, can have no hold upon an atheist." [41] Thus atheists, like "papists," are unfitted by their own beliefs to make good citizens of the City Locke has built. But the government of that City cannot reasonably demand other conformity of faith.

Aside from the negative objection to persecution, that what one citizen considers sure knowledge another will hold to be only another opinion no better than his own; Locke also asserted, less clearly or forcefully than Plato, the positive need for dialectic if truth is to abound. John Milton in his *Areopagitica* has seen both points. "And he who were pleasantly disposed," Milton had written bitingly of censorship of the press, "could not well avoid to liken it to the exploit of that gallant man who thought to pound up the crows by shutting his park gate." [42] So much for the negative point. But as for the positive point, the human need for dialectical refutation, Milton feared "a gross conforming stupidity, a stark and dead congealment of wood and hay and stubble, forced and frozen together, which is more to the sudden degenerating of a Church than many sub-dichotomies of petty schisms." [43]

Locke, too, bases toleration on this positive need

for refutation. For "the business of laws is not to provide for the truth of opinions, but for the safety and security of the commonwealth, and of every particular man's goods and person. And so it ought to be. For the truth certainly would do well enough if she were once left to shift for herself. She seldom has received, and I fear never will receive, much assistance from the power of great men, to whom she is but rarely known, and more rarely welcome. She is not taught by laws, nor has she any need of force to procure her entrance into the minds of men. Errors indeed prevail by the assistance of foreign and borrowed succours. But if Truth makes not her way into the understanding by her own light, she will be but the weaker for any borrowed force violence can add to her." [44]

Locke wanted the City of Man to save man from political oppression and restore to him the right he had chiefly enjoyed in the state of Nature: freedom. To restore and to render even securer than it could be in the state of Nature. The political community could hope to serve no higher purpose than this highly personal right of each individual man. With that right secured, each man could be trusted to find, by his own efforts and his own choice of means, whatever happiness he might be destined to attain.

Hobbes, who feared anarchy, defended the omnipotence of the government against the individual. Locke, who feared tyranny, defended against tyrannical government the natural right of the individual to freedom. Montesquieu, in effect, rejoins to both: it depends on what sort of individuals you are dealing with. Montesquieu knows about abstract human nature; for that very reason he begins *The Spirit of Laws* with a discussion of what law is in the abstract, what natural law is, what the law of nations is—all this in the great tradition of the Greeks and of the Christian theologians. But the bulk of his work is an exposition of what kinds of laws are relevant to different kinds of men. He notes that the principle, the spring, the motive force, the driving power of republican government, is "political virtue," which he defines as a love of country and a love of equality. This kind of virtue enables a people to govern itself. If the government is democratic in form, this political virtue must be extremely widespread. If it is aristocratic, obviously it need exist less widely.

The spring or driving force that will make monarchy work is love of honor based on ambition. Not much political virtue is required.

The driving power of despotic government is fear. In a despotism, political virtue in the subject is unnecessary and honor or ambition is positively dangerous.

It follows that a different type of education is needed to support each of these different types of government. And different kinds of laws should be made by each.

Montesquieu attacks Hobbes for supposing that justice is irrelevant until government has been set up. Nor does he think it is man's desire to dominate what drives him to seek the shelter of government. It is, he says, man's natural desire for peace. His other natural desires include the desire for food, the desire to associate with other human beings (which includes the sexual desire), and his desire to know, which drives him to co-operate with other men. It is after he has obeyed the natural laws which derive from these four basic desires of his nature that a state of war begins. He then seeks government.

But what kind of government he will seek depends on a multitude of material circumstances: climate, soil, geographical location, methods of production, customs, manners. And Montesquieu supports this point—a thoroughly Platonic and Aristotelian point —by a more extensive survey of historical and anthropological data than either Plato or Aristotle had the means of conducting. Although he obviously admires republican government, although he obviously despises despotism, he is coolly observing that few populations have ever been competent to govern themselves; that most have been able to live under constitutional monarchy; and that some will obey only a despot. And the spirit in which each of these types of government can, and should, legislate will differ with the type of population to be governed and with the type of government to be rendered stable and effective.

The conversation about the City of Man which we have been following, like the earlier conversations about the Dialectical Republic and about the City of God, has been a conversation about human happiness; about what individual human acts or thoughts conduce to that happiness; about what political arrangements conduce to it; and what property rights in the material basis for human life are proper to that life. Because individual human acts and political enactments and economic agreements alike involve choosing, or trying to choose, between good and evil, the problem of the human will has run through this conversation. With Rousseau the problem of the will becomes suddenly much more acute. Machiavelli and Hobbes had concerned themselves primarily with how the prince, or sovereign government, can make its will prevail. Spinoza rejects the idea that the human will is free at all, and tries to teach us how to understand necessity and find happiness in it. Locke not only accepts free will but seeks those political devices that will give to the individual's will the maximum of freedom, that will enlarge the scope of its operation, and above all protect it from the force of arbitrary government.

These solutions are alike in subordinating the science of theology in varying ways to the science of politics or government. Machiavelli is merely ironical about religion, and even ethics, and more than ironical about princes who claim to act religiously or ethically. Hobbes regards religion as necessarily a department of state: the state cannot hope to stand firm unless it limits men's opinions as well as their acts, which, after all, are ultimately based on their opinions. Spinoza makes religion a private affair, which effectually leaves politics in control of what is social. Locke wants his state to guarantee freedom of religion, although he cannot ask it to accept in a citizen loyalty to a spiritual head who is also a temporal, foreign prince, nor can he ask his state to tolerate citizens who knock out the underpinning from all government by denying the existence of God.

Rousseau does something quite different. In *The*

Social Contract he elevates the will of the whole community—the "general will," as he calls it—to the position of supremacy which Augustine or Thomas would have assigned only to the will of God. And the individual is expected to submit his will to that general will with something of the same joyful self-abnegation the Christian felt when he submitted to God's will—and only then. Hobbes does not require that of us: he asks us not to adore the sovereign but to fear and obey him absolutely. Locke requires the sovereign to let us alone as far as possible, so we can be free to choose what we will love. But Rousseau demands that we love the sovereign and tries to guarantee that the sovereign will be lovable by making sure he is not Hobbes's irresponsible government, but Locke's responsible one. For Locke's urbane acceptance of government as a necessary nuisance, Rousseau substitutes an ecstatic, patriotic devotion. We lose our individual freedom of will in order to find it, and find it in a higher form: participation in the general will of our community. Thus men once tried to lose their individual wills in God's will. To Rousseau the state—the self-governing, free state—is a moral entity whose service is perfect freedom. No wonder he holds that "the most general will is always the most just also, and that the voice of the people is in fact the voice of God." [45] Man, he says, in the state of Nature is not the arrogant, shrewd, dangerous animal that Hobbes portrayed, nor the good-natured but self-seeking reasoner Locke exhibits, but a creature with two governing passions: self-preservation and compassion. Man naturally loves his neighbor.

113

"The fundamental problem" of government, says Rousseau in *The Social Contract,* is how the individual can pass from the state of Nature to civil society without losing his personal freedom. " 'The problem is to find a form of association which will defend and protect with the whole common force the person and goods of each associate, and in which each, while uniting himself with all, may still obey himself alone, and remain as free as before.' This is the fundamental problem of which *The Social Contract* provides the solution." [46]

The solution? " *'Each of us puts his person and all his power in common under the supreme direction of the general will, and, in our corporate capacity, we receive each member as an indivisible part of the whole.'* " [47] What results, he continues, was formerly called a city and is now called a republic or body politic.

This somewhat mysterious "general will," Rousseau assures us, automatically seeks the common good of the community. It is arrived at by majority vote. May it not err? Yes, in practice, because the people may be deceived as to what in a specific instance will serve the common good. Nevertheless, it is the common good which the people always wills. Abstractly considered, therefore, the general will is infallible. Rousseau is here saying for the community what Plato said for the individual: that no man wittingly chooses evil. But where Plato was chiefly concerned with the means of enlightening the will by knowledge, Rousseau's attention is on the will, on desire, on emotion. This is why, in place of Hobbes's truculent cynicism, or Machiavelli's detached irony, or Locke's moderate and restrained and polite prose, Rousseau's literary style is passionate, emphatic, and at times sentimental. Compared with any of these others, Rousseau attaches enormous importance to what he feels, and to human feelings in general.

But although he counts heavily on friendship as the basis for good government and good laws, Rousseau is no fool. He has already insisted that man by nature is moved by self-preservation as well as by compassion for other men. He is anxious that neither the will of the individual citizen nor the corporate will of some group of citizens, some "interest" as we would say, shall deflect the general will of the whole electorate from its proper goal: the common good. Therefore, where Locke opens the door wide to individual wealth, Rousseau is quick to announce that "laws are always of use to those who possess and harmful to those who have nothing; from which it follows that the social state is advantageous to men only when all have something and none too much." [48] So long as the function of the general will is not usurped by these particular wills, it is idle to ask "whether the law can be unjust, since no one is unjust to himself; nor how we can be both free and subject to the laws, since they are but registers of our wills." [49]

Given these views, we shall not be surprised to find Rousseau advocating what most contemporary Americans, nurtured in the tradition of Lockean individualism, will consider socialistic. For instance, Locke lauds the invention of money precisely because it permits the individual to convert "perishable" surplus, which could be justly claimed by the community if it started to go to waste, into money capital, which we have a natural right to keep and even to pass on to our heirs. Rousseau, on the contrary, deeply distrusts money as a constantly corrupting influence that competes with freedom as the object of our love. For this reason, taxes look to him like bribes which the citizens give the government to get government to take off their hands the bother of serving the common good. Forced labor, provided only it be the general will that commands it, Rousseau therefore finds less opposed to liberty than taxes are.

It is tempting for the free citizen of the Locke variety, with his profound distrust of "government interference," to smell in Rousseau's writings a dangerous state-idolatry, much more dangerous than Hobbes's idolatry because it is a kind of self-idolatry, an idolatry of something we have ourselves created. And it is even more tempting for those who have so loudly clamored for "free enterprise" to fear the socialistic strain in Rousseau and his hatred of private interests parading as the common good. But it is not easy to deny that the common good does, in fact, transcend in importance the good, or at least the material good, of an individual, or even the good of a modern business corporation. If it does not, how dare we conscript men to risk their lives defending their political community; and how dare we demand of a business corporation that it obtain a charter? And what will, other than the general will, can justly send a man to the battle front or dictate the conditions under which a corporation will be allowed to operate?

It is tempting to a Christian to insist that God's will is above all human wills, even the general will. But Rousseau might answer that in political matters, which are human matters, God's will must be looked for in some human will. What he is looking for is the source of political authority; and if he asks you where else except in his "general will" it is to be found, he will not be put off with the reply, "God knows." He would probably admit that God knew, but he would like to know how a man can know. Does God's will pass direct from God to the individual voter's conscience? Watch out that the voter is not hearing one of Rousseau's "corporate" wills—the will, for instance, of one of our modern corporations, seeking not the common good of the state but the profit of the shareholders—or perhaps next year's bonus for the officers of the corporation. If God's voice is to be detected in the voice of some group of human beings, such as a church that professes to have as its mission the transmittal to men of the commands of God, Rousseau will start smelling another corporate good. Thus Rousseau classifies "Roman Christianity" with the religion of the Lamas which gives men "two codes of legislation, two rulers, and two countries" [50]—Locke's objection to Roman Catholicism. Nor does Rousseau think Christians in general have made good citizens, precisely because "the country of the Christian is not of this world."

To the thorny problem of Church and State, Rousseau offers as drastic a solution as does Hobbes. Indeed it is in essence the same solution: the sovereign fixes the religion, a religion that promotes the common good of the society. But with this important difference: in Rousseau the sovereign can never be less than the whole political society. In short, for Rousseau religious dogma is subject to the general will. *The Social Contract* culminates, therefore, in a chapter with the bold title, "Civil Religion," in which he declares:

"There is therefore a purely civil profession of faith of which the Sovereign should fix the articles, not exactly as religious dogmas, but as social sentiments without which a man cannot be a good citizen or a faithful subject. While it can compel no one to believe them, it can banish from the State whoever does not believe them—it can banish him, not for impiety, but as an anti-social being, incapable of truly loving the laws and justice, and of sacrificing, at need, his life to his duty. If any one, after publicly recognizing these dogmas, behaves as if he does not believe them, let him be punished by death: he has committed the worst of all crimes, that of lying before the law.

"The dogmas of civil religion ought to be few, simple, and exactly worded, without explanation or commentary. The existence of a mighty, intelligent and beneficent Divinity, possessed of foresight and providence, the life to come, the happiness of the just, the punishment of the wicked, the sanctity of the social contract and the laws: these are its positive dogmas. Its negative dogmas I confine to one, intolerance, which is a part of the cults we have rejected." [51]

I set out just now with Rousseau in search of a political state in which I would be truly free and I wind up now in a church-state with a religious test for citizens. If I do not believe "the dogmas of civil religion," I shall be excommunicated—quite literally, for I shall be banished. I shall be banished if I do not believe in the existence of God, in immortality of the soul, in the rewards and punishments of the life to come. At least, I shall be if my fellow-citizen Rousseau can persuade the majority of our other fellow-citizens that the general will ought to will that these dogmas are correct. If, to avoid this nasty situation, I say I accept these dogmas and am then thought to act as if I did not, I shall be put to death. Although the general will, if Rousseau persuades it, sternly forbids me to be intolerant, its love of tolerance will not prevent the general will itself from either banishing me out of my country or putting me to death if I do not believe what it wills to be "the dogmas of civil religion," which fortunately or unfortunately as one may judge the matter, are "few, simple, and exactly worded." For the general will, as ascertained somewhat uncertainly by the majority vote of my neighbors, is by definition infallible. The City of Man, as reconnoitered by Rousseau, can be a very tough place for a fellow of wavering faith to live in.

One of the more alarming characteristics of Rousseau's City of Man is that the contemporary name for its "civil religion" is nationalism. Now, nationalism can certainly rise to a kind of ecstasy that transcends personal egoism and it can lead to heroic acts

of sacrifice. But among its numerous ugly characteristics is the brutal fact that it is exclusive. Leviathan
still reserves the right to make war on other Levia-
thans. My natural compassion for my fellowmen has
received political expression so far as Rousseau's social contract extends—that is, to the other citizens
of my own state. But "truly loving the laws" of my
own state has a horrid way of inducing me to loathe
the laws of foreign states. And Rousseau's ideal state
is a pretty small affair. He agrees with Montesquieu
that republican government is difficult for a large
state. If "the most general will is always the most
just also"; if the general will of the whole state is
therefore juster than the "corporate will" of a business or of a church or of some other lesser social
group; ought not the general will of all mankind to
be considerably juster than the general will of one
of mankind's many sovereign states? For the general
will of a national state is with respect to the general
will of mankind, a kind of "corporate will," a kind
of special group interest—or would be, if only all
mankind would enter a social contract to govern itself. But, as Rousseau suggests, is not all mankind
too big a group to do this effectively?

Rousseau perceived this problem. In the second
chapter of the original draft of his *Social Contract*
he expressed the possibility of a moral entity even
higher than the general will of any existing state:
"the federation of the world." And at the end of
Book III, Chapter XV, of the work as published, he
writes: "I will show later on how the external
strength of a great people may be combined with
the convenient polity and good order of a small

State." [52] In a footnote to this sentence he adds: "I had intended to do this in the sequel to this work, when in dealing with external relations I came to the subject of confederations. The subject is quite new, and its principles have still to be laid down." [53] And there the matter is dropped.

Rousseau's *Discourse on the Origin of Inequality* and his *Discourse on Political Economy* throw additional light on the political theory in *The Social Contract*. Inequality among men has arisen with the essential artificiality of civilized and political existence. In the state of Nature, which he eloquently praises, men were equal and lived a good life. Savages, he insists, never commit suicide. But as population threatened subsistence, this idyllic state gave way before property rights. With these rights Rousseau is, as usual, less favorably impressed than Locke. "The first man," he writes, "who, having enclosed a piece of ground, bethought himself of saying *This is mine*, and found people simple enough to believe him, was the real founder of civil society." [54] He thinks it would have been lucky if some other man had immediately pulled up the stakes of this claimant and had denounced him as an impostor. With the rise of property came law. Then came magistrates to administer the law. Then the magistrates converted their legal function into arbitrary rule. All the inequalities that followed, says Rousseau, are ultimately reducible to the difference between rich and poor. When wealth and poverty have been duly concentrated and tyranny reigns, men are really back in a state of Nature, but in a corrupt form of that state. It is only the restoration of law that rescues us from that second and degraded state of Nature. As to law, there is a suggestion of Spinoza's admiration for the general and hence necessary. It is the glory of law that it is general, where despotic decrees are particular and specific. Law is, indeed, "the most sublime of all human institutions, or rather . . . a divine inspiration." It imitates "the unchangeable decrees of the Deity." [55]

There is light on the mysterious "general will." Why does Rousseau put the emphasis on the will rather than on the intellect, which is where the Greek and Christian traditions had put it? In Plato's political society the power that locates the common good is the understanding. It is reason, acting primarily through the guardians, that rules the Republic. The problem is to see the good; once seen, it is certain to be willed by those who see it. Rousseau himself pictures the general will as having for its fixed object the common good. But it is the willing, not the thinking, that interests Rousseau, as it interested Locke. Locke sang a paean to freedom, because he wanted his individual citizen to possess as many choices as possible. Politics is deliberating and choosing, not speculating and knowing. It is the will that chooses. Rousseau submits a curious piece of evidence to support this emphasis on the will. Animals, he assures us, have ideas. Man differs from animals not by virtue of unique intellectual powers but by virtue of free will. Why animals, if in fact they do entertain ideas, should always act by instinct rather than by reason Rousseau does not make clear, except by admitting that man differs from other animals by the degree of intellectuality he possesses. Traditionally, free will had been assumed to be the choosing power of what has the ideas: the intellect. In short, will depended on reason. But somehow this connection seems not to impress Rousseau, and man comes out to be, not so much the one animal that thinks, as the one animal that wills. When he associates with his fellows, it is perhaps natural, therefore, that the chief product of the association should be the general will, rather than the community of understanding towards which the Dialectical Republic of Plato constantly strove. This voluntarism, this emphasis on the human will, we shall meet again as the City of Man expands and waxes stronger.

The underlying faith in Gibbon's *Decline and Fall of the Roman Empire* is the underlying faith of Locke's *Second Treatise of Civil Government*: that political freedom for the individual, and the civil institutions that promote and secure it, is the ultimate basis for human happiness and for social progress alike. But Gibbon is also as sure as Montesquieu that if political freedom fosters virtue, virtue is also the necessary condition of free political institutions. Gibbon is one of the world's great ironists. He is ironical about religion, about military glory, about politics; but he is never ironical about liberty. In the decline of Rome he always sees, under the surface phenomena, the decline of liberty. His great and compendious work, recording the history both of the Empire and its neighbors for a span

of thirteen centuries, from the peaceful period of
the Antonines to the fall of Constantinople, follows
the same basic theme as the last section of Herodotus's *History* of the Persian War: how a wise, temperate, courageous, just society may debauch itself
through conquest, wealth, and tyranny, first into a
menagerie of vicious animals and finally into ruin.

Gibbon knew that he had found a subject fit for
an historian: the collapse of an entire civilization.
It was uniquely fit, for Graeco-Roman civilization
was the only civilization about which Gibbon's generation possessed enough data to furnish the picture
of such a collapse. He had conceived the idea of nar-
rating so majestic and terrible a story as the fall of
the City of Man "amidst the ruins of the Capitol,"
and his opening paragraph proclaims that what he
has to talk about is important to the reader:

"In the second century of the Christian era, the
Empire of Rome comprehended the fairest part of
the earth, and the most civilised portion of mankind. The frontiers of that extensive monarchy were
guarded by ancient renown and disciplined valour.
The gentle but powerful influence of laws and manners had gradually cemented the union of the prov-
inces. Their peaceful inhabitants enjoyed and
abused the advantages of wealth and luxury. The
image of a free constitution was preserved with decent reverence: the Roman senate appeared to possess the sovereign authority, and devolved on the
emperors all the executive powers of government.
During a happy period (A.D. 98–180) of more than
fourscore years, the public administration was con-
ducted by the virtue and abilities of Nerva, Trajan,

Hadrian, and the two Antonines. It is the design of this, and of the two succeeding chapters, to describe the prosperous condition of their empire; and afterwards, from the death of Marcus Antoninus, to deduce the most important circumstances of its decline and fall; a revolution which will ever be remembered, and is still felt by the nations of the earth." [56]

In these balanced sentences with their balanced adjectives; in this deliberate cadence; in this elegant, sophisticated, Latinized English; the work continues for seventy-one unhurried and judicious chapters. Their author was an ironical Epicurean who desired, to use one of his own favorite expressions, to be both "amusing and instructive," and his desire was fully and pleasantly attained. Human folly, of which he had much to record, did not call out the denunciation, the indignation of a Rousseau, but an irony generally gay, occasionally cutting. For example, comparing the younger Gordian with his father, he observes: "His manners were less pure, but his character was equally amiable with that of his father. Twenty-two acknowledged concubines, and a library of sixty-two thousand volumes, attested the variety of his inclinations, and from the productions which he left behind him, it appears that the former as well as the latter were designed for use rather than ostentation." [57] Again, expressing polite incredulity at the common Christian estimates of the number of martyrs who fell in the persecutions of Diocletian and his successors, Gibbon indulges in some disinterested calculation and allows "an annual consumption of one hundred and fifty martyrs."

For Gibbon dislikes the early Christians, whom he finds enthusiastic, strident, vulgar, ignorant, and superstitious. Also, like Rousseau, he finds them bad citizens, who contributed directly to the decline of that elegant City of Man, over which the mild Antonines were discovered reigning in the opening paragraph of his great work. That City continues to shine through the pages of *The Decline and Fall,* though more and more dimly as Roman virtue degenerates into luxury, cowardice, and sloth. It is a City whose citizens are free men; reasonable, moderate, admirers of all that is ordered according to Nature but admirers with a decent reverence for a somewhat vague and somewhat functionless Deity. In such a City a prudent man could find much to enjoy and some things worth lamenting, if he knew with any certainty of a better City and if lamenting did aught to soften his lot in this one.

The ethical writing of Kant will recall us to the teasing problem of the will. Take, for instance, *The Fundamental Principles of the Metaphysics of Ethics.* In this brief work Kant is looking for clearly recognizable first principles to guide human conduct. He finds such a principle, not in what we desire or love, not in any sort of reward, but in duty. And that duty expresses itself in what Kant terms the Categorical Imperative as distinguished from the Hypothetical Imperative. The hypothetical imperative tells our reason that we must perform such and such acts if we would achieve such and such purposes. But it does not test the purposes. On the other hand, the categorical imperative does not base the command of conscience on any subjective purpose but on an objective necessity higher than our individual predilections. *"Act only on that maxim which will enable you at the same time to will that it be a universal law."* [58] This categorical imperative, Kant holds, applies to any rational being and hence to man. Kant, like Plato, finds certainty and consistency only in the invisible world of reason and intellect. The phenomenal world, the world of appearances, Plato's world of "becoming," is not only confused; ultimately it is unknowable to us, except as our ideas seem to fit its phenomena. If we would not base conduct on confusion, we must turn back from that confused world of sense impressions and imagination to the clear world of concepts, back from the world of the contingent to the world of the necessary, back from the particular to the universal. In that invisible, universal, and necessary world we will apprehend directly the truth of the categorical imperative, although the limitations of human reason will not permit us to know why it is true. Kant considers the Christian Golden Rule "trivial," compared with this categorical imperative. It is not a question of acting towards my neighbor as I would *like* to have him act towards me. It is not a *quid pro quo,* a bargain. It is that I *ought* to act in such a fashion that I recognize my act as intelligible. This necessary and intelligible world of concepts was for Spinoza, too, the source of good and wise action, although of course both Kant and Spinoza—and indeed any intelligent person—know that the practical application of the guidance we get from that source calls for prudence and experience and is subject to countless errors.

Was it with some glimpse of this principle in mind that Rousseau felt so confident of the worth and validity of the general will? Kant finds an act free if, instead of being based on external compulsion or even on the compulsion our own desires impose on us, it is based on our understanding of universals; and he holds that our mind insists on the validity of the categorical imperative. We are free when, in willing an act, we are legislating universally: our will is then "giving itself the law." A will thus free cannot base its choice on one of the special interests that Rousseau so properly dreaded. This is why Rousseau so rightly insisted that there can be no general will directed to a particular object. It is because law is general and not particular that it is the most sublime of all human institutions. It is because it turns for guidance to Kant's and Spinoza's realm of the necessary that it reminds Rousseau of "the unchangeable decrees of the Deity." And is this not also why he holds "that the most general will is always the most just also, and that the voice of the people is in fact the voice of God"? [59]

Rousseau's *Social Contract* sought an ethical basis for government, so that a man might truly remain free while obeying law. And Kant, seeking an ultimate basis for doing one's individual duty, advises us to will only those personal acts which we would will the whole community to perform if we were "legislating" for the whole community. Kant, seeking the basis for ethics, finds it in an ideal government! Man has dignity for Kant precisely because he is free and makes laws (whether ethical or political) for himself and other men as "ends in themselves," never as means. This is why each rational being must act as though in his maxims he were at all times a legislating member in the universal realm of ends. It is this, Kant adds, that makes men "persons." Will not the grandeur of these Kantian concepts explain why Rousseau so passionately wills that in the political community the General Will must prevail—even over the natural right of Locke's citizen to convert "perishable" goods into imperishable capital?

But a strange paradox remains. As a citizen of Rousseau's City, I am promised freedom if I submit to the general will of the City. As a Kantian "person," I am promised freedom if I think of myself as legislating for all mankind, for all men in all Cities everywhere. How can my political conduct and my ethical conduct be brought into accord? Must I, to be a good citizen, be a bad man? Or can a City be built that shall include all men as citizens?

The key to such a City, capable of sheltering and freeing all mankind, is the Constitution of the United States, as analyzed in *The Federalist*.

How great a triumph of craftsmanship this key to the City is, will become apparent quickly enough if we glance back over the writings of the great political thinkers. Plato's dialectical republic maintained an army. Although the whole design of *The Republic* is the substitution of reason and law for whim and force, the philosopher king's writ does not run beyond the frontier of a very small state. The state is an island of men reasoning together and defending itself by force against a sea of foreigners beating against its embattled shores. Aristotle was insistent that if the citizen was to be free, if he was to obey only laws he had helped make, the City must be small. War is accepted by all men, even by the gods. Reason detests it, as Homer's Zeus declares Ares hateful. Aristophanes mocked its folly. Thucydides saw its tragedy, its futility, and its deep irony. Virgil glorified a peace the Roman had imposed after secular strife. Tacitus painted the horrors of that strife. But war was accepted by poet and philosopher alike as part of the glory and misery of man. Being rational, man was capable of law; being animal, he nevertheless prostituted his reason to violence and made war.

Augustine and Thomas admitted war as morally justifiable even for the City of God, whose mediator was the Prince of Peace. Though quarreling governments may appeal to the natural "law" of nations, there is no positive, humanly enforceable law above them, as there is above individuals in a lawful civil society. So there may be "just" war.

The City of Man received war as part of its inheritance from the Cities that preceded it. Machiavelli candidly analyzed war as an instrument of policy. Rabelais, like Aristophanes, brilliantly depicted its cruel absurdity. Hobbes gladly sacrificed political freedom to save man from the hell of civil war or anarchy and saw with bitter clarity that every sovereign government is essentially and constantly in a state of war with all other sovereign governments, whether declared war or undeclared, whether white war, gray war, or cold war. Diplomacy and espionage take up when armies recess. Locke knows government must possess a power called "federative," by which he simply means "the power of war and peace, leagues and alliances, and all the transactions with all the persons and communities without the commonwealth." [60] But these transactions, even when not violent, obviously have no ultimate human sanction except violence. Rousseau, like Aristotle, believed his state must be small if it was to be self-governing. But he knew that smallness spelled military weakness. He had hoped to deal with "the subject of confederations. The subject is quite new, and its principles have still to be laid down." [61] Gibbon sadly recognized that the Rome of his beloved Antonines had long since lost the freedom enjoyed by the politically virtuous citizens of the young and tiny Roman Republic. But he was awed by the majesty of an area of law and reason that had salvaged from an ocean of barbarism and violence "the fairest part of the earth, and the most civilized portion of mankind." Of all these writers, Montesquieu alone discerned the sort of key that would open the City of Man to both freedom and peace, that would extend the franchise of citizen to that most paradoxical of outlaws: the man outside the law merely because he is outside the city wall. The key, says Montesquieu, is a confederate republic.

"This form of government is a convention by which several petty states agree to become members of a larger one, which they intend to establish. It is a kind of assemblage of societies, that constitute a new one, capable of increasing, by means of further associations, till they arrive at such a degree of power as to be able to provide for the security of the whole body. . . .

"A republic of this kind, able to withstand an external force, may support itself without any internal corruption . . ." [62]

Montesquieu had seen that a key must be found; he had even described it in broad outline. But at Philadelphia, in the summer of 1787, a small group of delegates from twelve of the thirteen sovereign and independent states on the long Atlantic shore of a new world sweated patiently and courageously over the hot forge of political debate and wrought the key that Montesquieu foresaw. At Philadelphia, whose name auspiciously signified brotherly love, the Founding Fathers of the American Union drafted the Constitution of the United States.

The Declaration of Independence, which will be quickly recognized as pure John Locke, had severed the thirteen colonies from their British sovereign. The Articles of Confederation had united them in "a firm league of friendship with each other," a league not unlike the late League of Nations or the present United Nations. Article II guaranteed to each league member its sovereignty, as Article II of the United Nations Charter does today. But the Constitution drafted at Philadelphia provided not for a league but for a government, a government that would be common to all the citizens of all the states that might ratify it. Although unlike the earlier Articles, the new Constitution did not specifically invite Canada to join, it was so devised that the new states which were expected to form in the West could be admitted on equal terms with the founding states. The new Union was, to use Montesquieu's phrase, "a kind of assemblage of societies, that constitute a new one, capable of increasing, by means of further associations . . ." [63] Indeed, although few Americans reflect upon the fact, there was not only nothing whatever in the Constitution to prevent the American Union from admitting Hawaii or Alaska; there is nothing to prevent its admitting Great Britain or France. There is no limit whatever in theory to the number of states it can incorporate, precisely because it is based on, and expresses, absolutely universal principles. In theory, the only qualification for admission is that the applying state must have "a republican form of government."

It was this Constitution that Hamilton, Madison, and Jay set out to defend in a series of brief essays known as *The Federalist,* published in various New York newspapers, addressed "to the People of the State of New York," and designed to persuade that sovereign people to ratify the Constitution now submitted and thereby to establish with the citizens of other ratifying states a common government, while retaining their own government for all the purposes it was fitted to perform.

The Constitution that New York finally ratified has stood the test of time; it is the oldest written constitution operative in the world today. For that fact, however, the American people have many circumstances to thank: the isolation of the country till it had reached great strength, the well-nigh boundless natural resources at their disposal, the wise statesmanship of at least some of their political leaders.

The American people have perhaps made only two major contributions to the civilization of mankind, and the federal theory exemplified in the Constitution and expounded in *The Federalist* is the greater of those two. The other major contribution, surely, is mass production, whether industrial or agricultural. It is true, as we have just recalled, that a Frenchman had enunciated the federal theory in rough; indeed, *The Federalist* appeals to his authority. It is true also that the industrial revolution was born in England and developed on the continent of Europe before it spread to America. But the Constitution and *The Federalist* went so much further than Montesquieu, and American industrial organization so much further than British or Continental, that it remains perhaps true that these two contributions—federalism in the field of political science and, in the economic area, mass production—are American. The federal principle welcomes all mankind to the franchise of a universal free city, surely the City of Man in its fairest form. Mass production insistently—and to many Americans, frighteningly —invites all men to economic freedom. On this subject we shall hear later from Karl Marx.

At their noblest, the Constitution and *The Federalist* summon all men everywhere to live reasonably as "legislating members in the universal realm of ends," as ends in themselves; that is, free persons with dignity and an understanding of duty. But they summon all men with the most extraordinary, clear-sighted awareness that man is not only rational but animal. He cannot find happiness, therefore, without the freedom that Locke and Rousseau alike demand and that Montesquieu and even Machiavelli prefer where obtainable. But man is also an animal and therefore subject to appetites and passions, which law—that is, reason backed up by the ultimate sanction of force—must help his mind to control; without strong government he falls into the anarchy which Hobbes so clearly and fearfully beheld. *The Federalist* therefore presented the Constitution as a cunning device for filtering off, as it were, the passions, and leaving the reason free to deliberate on the common good that the general will necessarily seeks. The separation of powers, which Locke and Montesquieu alike extolled, favors this filtering device, promotes disinterested deliberation, and helps the citizen distinguish in practice between functions of government that are clearly distinguishable in theory. The limitation of terms of office helps him distinguish between the formal powers of an office and the particular man that accidentally exercises those formal, permanent, and necessary powers.

Much of the reasoning in *The Federalist* is the sort of *ad hoc* reasoning into which the Anglo-Saxon so readily falls. Much of it makes an appeal to history for precedents, as a common-law advocate might appeal. But the appeal is never to rule of thumb; it is always the double appeal to reason and experience, to what clearly accords with abstract knowledge and to what appears to agree with the nature of the world of sense. For man is both rational and animal, and he operates in both eternity and time.

This awareness of man's double nature protects both the Constitution and *The Federalist* from a foolish idealism on the one hand and a cheap cynicism on the other. The awareness is both pride and humility: pride when it recalls man's reason, his freedom, his responsibility; humility when it remembers his frailties, his appetites, his passions, and even the fallibility of his merely human reason. Neither document exhibits, therefore, the oscillation between soft-headed sentimentality and "getting tough" that our own generation so frequently exhibits. But political wisdom might, after all, have been exhibited in some other kind of constitution than a federal one. The true subtlety of the American Constitution and the true subtlety of *The Federalist* lie in the device of "concurrent jurisdiction." This device permits each member-state of a federal union to exercise most of the powers of the sovereign while allocating certain specified powers to the union government. If it be objected that Rousseau has already demonstrated that sovereignty is indivisible, *The Federalist* can reply: since "the people" is the sovereign, it is up to them whether they wish a given governmental power to be exercised through their local state government or through the federal government. But which people? "The People of the State of New York" to whom *The Federalist* addressed its arguments? Or of Virginia? Or Pennsylvania? Or is "the people" the population of the thirteen states, taken indiscriminately? The Preamble to the Constitution appears to say the latter, since it states that "We, the People of the United States . . . do ordain and establish this Constitution . . ." [64] But the Constitution as drafted, Preamble and all, was not submitted to majority vote of that sovereign people, but to thirteen separate sovereign peoples acting through their respective ratifying conventions. The Charter of the United Nations, though it self-consciously apes the American Preamble, carefully and quite logically changes the famous phrase to "We the Peoples." This change makes the Charter what it genuinely is, a joint declaration by a number of sovereigns, relinquishing none of that sovereignty. With equal logic the Constitution of the United States does not explicitly mention the sovereignty of the individual states. Could we persuade Rousseau to admit that thirteen sovereign peoples, acting through their respective ratifying conventions, dissolved their thirteen respective social compacts and simultaneously entered a single and larger social compact, under which they agreed to delegate—rather than "leave" —many powers of government in the hands of the thirteen original governments?

There is no evidence that the Founding Fathers recognized this metaphysical refinement. Perhaps some pale reflection of the difficulty expressed itself in the misgivings many persons felt as to how the delegations from twelve states—Rhode Island had not sent delegates—could transcend their authority, which was actually to agree to improvements in a league of sovereigns, and to set up a new sovereign. Legalistic though the point may be, it contributed heavily seventy-four years later to a bloody Civil

War—and still makes some people prefer to call that war the War Between the States.

Whatever sleight of hand was worked, whether at Philadelphia or in the various state conventions; however instinctive and inexplicit the practical outcome; the working arrangement that emerged left most of the attributes of sovereignty to the states that had previously exercised them, and accorded a few important and necessary ones to the new common government which their respective sovereign governments had elected to set up. Above all, the new government was a real government; it was not a league, not a multilateral treaty between governments. And *The Federalist* is perfectly clear how this fact may be immediately known: the new government acts on individual citizens, not merely on component states. When the Congress raises money, it does not do it as the United Nations does it: by assessing contributions from member-states. It levies taxes on individuals, including of course such legal "persons" as corporations, and the executive branch collects these taxes. When the Congress makes a law, it is a real law applying to individual citizens, not merely a hopeful rule of conduct that member-states are morally obligated to follow. The Congress is not a diplomatic assembly, like the United Nations General Assembly, that makes agreements between member-states. It is a legislative assembly that makes those special rules that men call law, and it makes them for human beings. The United Nations General Assembly can act on its sovereign members, in the last analysis, only by making war on them. That is, it can keep the peace only by making war! The

Founding Fathers had observed this same absurdity
under the Articles of Confederation and had decided that a government over governments is a monstrosity. Government deals with persons. So the new
Constitution authorized the Federal government to
punish persons. Or, more briefly, it replaced a
league that called itself a government, with a government that really was a government.

The jurisdiction of the new government and the
jurisdiction of the local state government are concurrent, and are distinguished from each other in
the Constitution. If Federal and state government
dispute jurisdiction, appeal is to the Supreme Court
of the Federal Government. The citizen of the component state therefore elects two sets of officials,
obeys two sets of laws, pays two sets of taxes: state
and Federal. As a practical matter, this could scarcely
seem strange to communities whose political customs were of English origin and who were accustomed to a measure of local self-government. But at
Philadelphia a group of delegates from the twelve
sovereign and independent states that had sent delegates agreed, after prolonged deliberation, that their
sovereign governments were not adequate to protect
the lives, the liberties, and the property of their citizens and ought to be supplemented by a government, common to all the citizens of all the states,
that could perform this first and most necessary task
of human government. It was a brilliant discovery.
It rescues the City of Man from a terrible paradox:
that men should live together in a political community, bound together in the freedom which only law
can bring; that other men should live similarly un-

der the protection of similar governments; and that each of these governments, whose supreme purpose is to substitute law for force, should be doomed to arm itself against its neighbor, to be constantly ready to use force against its neighbor, in order that each may protect the little island of human reason which it is morally bound to protect. The name of this paradox is of course War, as Thomas Hobbes had made clear.

We have seen a long line of thinkers—Greek, Christian, and humanist—accept this paradox of war, sometimes with a sense of tragedy and fate, sometimes with resignation, or with bitterness, or ridicule, or cynicism. And we have seen Rousseau and Montesquieu stir in their thought as if they would break the vicious circle. But it remained for those who wrought the Constitution of the United States and for those who penned *The Federalist* to defy what looked like fate and to show how a group of free political communities, by means of a subtle yet simple political invention, can vastly enlarge the area of freedom and reason, and within that vaster area can force itself to serve its master, reason. Within that area, the paradox of military force is transmuted into the rationality of police force. Within that now enlarged area, the legal murder called battle gives way to execution, or imprisonment, of the lawbreaker who has been convicted by due process of law.

Although men like Franklin knew what Rousseau knew—that federation is a universal principle as much as human reason is, and that the logical culmination of the deed done at Philadelphia was, to

use Rousseau's words, "the federation of the world"
—neither the Constitution nor *The Federalist* follows through. They were written to solve a particular problem in a particular time and place, and this
took all their courage and energy. They were concerned with other principles of government besides
the federal principle they had discovered. They
were concerned with the first ten amendments to
the Constitution, the so-called Bill of Rights, that
would guarantee that the Federal Union now established would be a Dialectical Republic, open to the
fruitful clash of opinion. Nor could it have easily
occurred to them to envisage extending the principle to further lands than those to the west which
they were busy colonizing, or perhaps to Canada, if
only because of the vastness of distances in their day.

Human governments, unlike Thomas's and
Dante's angelic hierarchy, operate not only in time
but in space. The time it took to traverse the distance between New Hampshire and Georgia,
whether by horse, stagecoach, or sailing vessel, was
one of the most compelling arguments men brought
against adoption of the new Constitution. To those
laggard means of transportation were added the
means of communication. With no radio to make
communication instantaneous throughout the
planet; with no airplanes to bring the law-maker
from the most distant land, or the paratrooper or
bomb from the remotest enemy base, it would have
been difficult to see in 1787 how a "federation of
the world" could govern itself if it wanted to, or
what danger would make it want to. Therefore,
although the key to the Great City of Man had

been forged, it was used to open only a portion of that City, though one that would one day stretch from sea to sea. And both Constitution and *Federalist* provided, as men had so often provided before them, for war.

The Fathers of the Constitution not only provided for the legalized violence of foreign war; they provided for the incipient violence between Plato's two cities in one, the rich and the poor. Hamilton, notably, thought it important that the rich should be in a position to prevent the violence that poverty naturally breeds. We should not, indeed, take literally in a contemporary sense his denunciation of "a democracy" as distinguished from "a republic," since he clearly states that by the first term he means a general assembly of the people in the ancient Athenian manner (the kind of polity Rousseau so ardently admired) and that by "republic" he meant one in which the laws were made by chosen representatives. And yet his denunciation is not wholly empty of contemporary meaning either: he feared demagogues. He feared that if the poor and ignorant were allowed to participate too much in government, they would elect to office men like Jefferson, Jackson, Lincoln, and Franklin Roosevelt. The Constitution nowhere repeats the ringing words of the Declaration of Independence: that "all men are created equal." It left each state the right to restrict suffrage. It even left to each state the matter of human slavery. A recent American historian taught a whole generation of Americans to believe that their Constitution was cunningly contrived to protect the vested interests of the rich, and the economic status of those who drafted it was carefully examined to prove this point.

It is not our business here to examine the motives of the men who wrote the books we are discussing. It is perfectly possible for a man to write, from bad motives, a book overflowing with important truths; and it is equally possible for a man to write, from the best of motives, a book abounding in folly and wickedness. Hamilton, whose motives have been peculiarly suspect to the present generation, properly invites his readers to examine the arguments advanced in the light of their own reason.

The truth is that both these documents are in the tradition of John Locke. They are directed towards preserving life, liberty, and property. They do not provide for the poor; they assume that only Nature and individual diligence can do that. They do not provide for the education without which neither Rousseau nor Montesquieu would expect republican government to endure. These two writers would have looked to private initiative, or local taxation, or perhaps to Jefferson's statewide support at most, to see that the citizen was internally free and therefore possessed of enough "political virtue" to meet the responsibilities of citizenship. In general, they assumed that the goodness of their Constitution, which all of them regarded anyhow as most imperfect, would depend on the goodness of the component states. And on the ticklish point of religion they went further even than John Locke: they forbade the Federal government to meddle with it.

Although the "general welfare" clause in the Preamble of the Constitution suggests the strong common purposes of Rousseau's general will, the main lines that the Constitution lays down and that *The Federalist* supports are the lines of a highly individualistic and competitive society. The Bill of Rights aims at this competition on the dialectical plane of opinion; the "checks and balances" between the three branches of government aim at it in the operation of government itself; the tearing down of tariff walls, built by the individual states, aims at it on the economic plane; and the abolition of the member-states' right to coin money further facilitates the competition of commodities. Common weights and measures, a common postal system, and reciprocal rights of citizenship all conduce to bring the goods and services of all men to a common market. If, in this general competition, the poor should find the going rough—well, in this new Lockean paradise there is even hope for the poor. If the rich have seized all the common property in the community, either by mixing their labor with it or by some more complicated process, there are always the beckoning Western lands, which represent a handsome slice of "the great common of the world." Let the poor but stake out a claim to a section of that fertile government land, mix their labor with it, and thereby convert it into private property. There in the great waiting West where, to use John Locke's words, "there is enough, and as good left in common for others," let the energy and intelligence of every man be released. Politically, this is the land of the free. Economically, it is the El Dorado of equal opportunity. The covered wagon will rattle past, the axe will ring, the plough will break the plain, the nugget will gleam, the rich oil will gush, and there will be scarce time to remember that, long ago in Philadelphia, men wrought such a small thing as a key, a key to the federation of the world, to the universal City of Man.

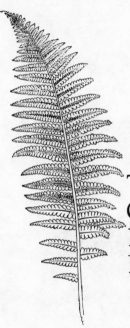

THE
GREAT
MERCANTILE
REPUBLIC

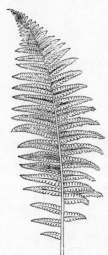

THE
GREAT
MERCANTILE
REPUBLIC

The year 1776 saw the publication of two related documents, the *Declaration of Independence* and Adam Smith's *Wealth of Nations*. Both vindicated the "natural rights" of man; but whereas the *Declaration* spoke more of political rights than economic ones, *The Wealth of Nations* is concerned primarily with man's natural right to buy and sell the fruits of his labor, unrestrained by government. Smith declares that "the propensity to truck, barter, and exchange . . . is common to all men, and to be found in no other race of animals, which seem to know neither this nor any other species of contracts." [65] Probably, he conjectures, it is the necessary consequence of the faculties of reason and speech.

The citizens of the Dialectical Republic are mutually dependent for the exchange of ideas, and through the clash of these ideas gain wisdom. Again, the citizens of the City of God are commanded to love God and one another, and through the loving mediation of Christ they attain to eternal happiness. The citizens of the City of Man covenant together to make law, and law shall make them free. The citizens of Adam Smith's "great mercantile republic" [66] exchange commodities, each with an eye to his own gain, and in this each is "led by an invisible hand to promote an end which was no part of his intention" [67]: the general prosperity of society. Man is a rational animal; man is a worshiping animal; man is a political animal; man is the buying and selling animal. He speaks, prays, makes law, trucks and barters. Men, therefore, assemble in the academy, in the church, in the forum, in the marketplace. *The Wealth of Nations* deals with the Marketplace.

Because man by nature trucks and barters, he early offered inducements to the special skills of his neighbors. The result was "the division of labour." [68] The man who hunted better than he fished, naturally trucked with the man who fished better than he hunted. Both got more, both of fish and game, by specializing. Plato had long ago noted this division of the arts among men and how the division leaves each worker free to perfect his special art. That was Plato's case for trained statesmen, trained soldiers, and trained craftsmen. Adam Smith specifies further. He notes that as the manual arts develop, as technology grows, division fruitfully continues. Fruitfully, for a number of reasons. Greater skill enormously increases output. No time becomes dead loss: "A man commonly saunters a little in turning his hand from one sort of employment to another." [69] Moreover, workmen who devote themselves exclusively to a single minute task seem more apt to invent labor-saving machines to help perform it faster or better. Even in the field of philosophy, Smith believes knowledge progresses much faster by dividing up the "fields" of knowledge. As specialization in manufacture increases, it reciprocally stimulates man's natural propensity to truck, barter, and exchange. For man's natural self-interest drives him always to buy cheap and sell dear.

Smith's insistence on man's natural self-interest will lead John Ruskin to speak of him as "the half-bred and half-witted Scotchman who taught the deliberate blasphemy: 'Thou shalt hate the Lord, thy God, damn his laws and covet his neighbor's goods.'" But Smith, like Hobbes, has a way of appealing to common experience. After describing man's life in a state of nature, or anarchy, as "solitary, poore, nasty, brutish, and short," Hobbes observes imperturbably: "It may seem strange to some man, that has not well weighed these things; that Nature should thus dissociate, and render men apt to invade, and destroy one another: and he may therefore, not trusting to this Inference, made from the Passions, desire perhaps to have the same confirmed by Experience. Let him therefore consider with himselfe, when taking a journey, he arms himselfe, and seeks to go well accompanied; when going to sleep, he locks his dores; when even in his house he locks his chests; and this when he knows there bee Lawes, and publike Officers, armed, to revenge all injuries shall bee done him; what opinion he has of his fellow subjects, when he rides armed; of his fellow Citizens, when he locks his dores; and of his children, and servants, when he locks his chests.

Does he not there as much accuse mankind by his actions, as I do by my words?" [70] And Smith appeals to the same sort of common observation of society and, indeed, of ourselves. He notes that "man has almost constant occasion for the help of his brethren, and it is in vain for him to expect it from their benevolence only. . . . It is not from the benevolence of the butcher, the brewer, or the baker that we expect our dinner, but from their regard to their own interest. We address ourselves, not to their humanity but to their self-love, and never talk to them of our own necessities but of their advantages. Nobody but a beggar chooses to depend chiefly upon the benevolence of his fellow-citizens." [71]

If men are "to help their brethren" through self-interest, there must be a place to truck and barter; there must be a Market-place. Without such a market the division of labor cannot grow. Lack of roads, waterways, or cities can prevent that market. Government interference, as in the case of protective tariffs, can prevent it. Even when it exists, it cannot flourish without a medium, as dialectic cannot flourish without the medium, the currency, of words. To be a good medium of exchange, this medium needs to be something everybody needs, and metal early turned out to be that thing. As Locke pointed out, it is imperishable, or nearly. It is also readily divisible. When it has been weighed, assayed, and stamped by an umpire government, the resultant coin is even more convenient than metal ingots. If the coin be of a scarce metal, like gold or silver, it avoids the bulkiness of a cheap metal and achieves the extra desirability of all scarce things. It is through this medium of money that men have come to truck, barter, exchange, and thereby help their brethren through self-interest.

Adam Smith seeks the rules men "naturally" observe when they buy and sell their property to each other: when they exchange goods for money, or goods for goods. These rules will determine the "exchangeable value" of things as against their use value, since some of the most useful things, like air and water, are in most places of no exchangeable value whatever. We need them more than the things we buy, but they are things, to use Hobbes's own expression, which God "freely giveth" rather than "for labour selleth to man-kind," and hence they have no market price.

But Smith wants to get behind the money price to the "real price" which that reflects; to determine this real price and discover its component parts. And he quickly agrees with Hobbes and Locke that "Labour was the first price, . . ."[72] Therefore, wealth is at bottom the command over labor. If I have money, I can in effect order other men to make things for me that I want, whether motorcars, clothes, or houses; or I can order them to wait on me, to doctor me, to teach me. I can, in short, buy either goods or services. This is the "power" of money, which so impressed Hobbes: command over the labor of other men.

To get this power of money the workman works; for a portion of that power he lays down a portion "of his ease, his liberty, and his happiness."[73]

The owner of "stock"—or, as we would say, the

capitalist—risks some of that stock to advance the workman's wage, to secure the raw material with which the workman is to mix his labor, and perhaps to buy tools for the workman. For risking his stock he will, if the venture succeeds, receive profit, or perhaps interest.

But no work can be done without a place to do it, and in fact the material worked on is often land, whether farm or mine. Once land has been taken up, the landlord will not allow it to be worked on without receiving rent.

The price of the finished product will be composed, then, of three parts: the workman's wage, the capitalist's profit, the landlord's rent. Each will get as much as he can; how much each can get will be governed by the supply of what he offers and the demand for what he offers. It is the Market-place which bribes each to contribute his effort to the common good, or at least to the common wealth, of mankind. It bribes the workman to barter his labor for wage; it bribes the capitalist to barter the use of his money for profit; it bribes the landlord to lend his land for rent.

"The produce of labour," says Smith, "constitutes the natural recompense or wages of labour.

"In that original state of things, which precedes both the appropriation of land and the accumulation of stock, the whole produce of labour belongs to the labourer. He has neither landlord nor master to share with him." [74]

But "As soon as land becomes private property, . . ." the landlord's rent "makes the first deduction . . ." [75] The profit of the person who advances the capital "makes a second deduction." The workmen will get what is left.

How much will be left? That will depend upon the contract between the workmen and the masters —the capitalists—"whose interests are by no means the same. The workmen desire to get as much, the masters to give as little as possible. The former are disposed to combine in order to raise, the latter in order to lower, the wages of labour.

"It is not, however, difficult to foresee which of the two parties must, upon all ordinary occasions, have the advantage in the dispute, and force the other into a compliance with their terms." [76] For in Smith's day the law allowed the masters to combine but strictly forbade the workmen to do so. Besides, "In all such disputes the masters can hold out much longer. A landlord, a farmer, a master manufacturer, a merchant, though they did not employ a single workman, could generally live a year or two upon the stocks which they have already acquired. Many workmen could not subsist a week, few could subsist a month, and scarce any a year without employment. In the long-run the workman may be as necessary to his master as his master is to him; but the necessity is not so immediate.

"We rarely hear, it has been said, of the combinations of masters, though frequently of those of workmen. But whoever imagines, upon this account, that masters rarely combine, is as ignorant of the world as of the subject. Masters are always and everywhere in a sort of tacit, but constant and uniform combination, not to raise the wages of labour above their

actual rate. To violate this combination is everywhere a most unpopular action, and a sort of reproach to a master among his neighbours and equals.
We seldom, indeed, hear of this combination, because it is the usual, and one may say, the natural
state of things, which nobody ever hears of." [77]

"Natural" as this sort of thing might be, Smith
obviously does not consider it natural in the same
sense as the free competition of masters for labor,
or of workmen for jobs. All monopoly is an interference with this natural propensity to buy cheap
and sell dear. He therefore detests the remains of
the guild system, the old corporations; he detests
"corporation laws and the corporation spirit." He
detests the apprentice system as a hypocritical and,
on the whole, inefficient method of exploiting the
apprentice. "People of the same trade seldom meet
together," he observes drily, "even for merriment
and diversion, but the conversation ends in a con-
spiracy against the public, or in some contrivance
to raise prices. It is impossible indeed to prevent
such meetings, by any law which either could be
executed, or would be consistent with liberty and
justice. But though the law cannot hinder people
of the same trade from sometimes assembling together, it ought to do nothing to facilitate such
assemblies, much less to render them necessary." [78]
Basically, Smith holds, monopoly is "violent," where
a really free trade in commodities is "natural."

The real cure for the disadvantage the wage-earner
is under is a "thriving" community, or as we would
say today, an expanding economy. Then the landlord and the capitalist compete for labor and wages

are run up "naturally." In any case, there is what we would call a floor under wages: workmen must be paid to enable them to subsist and to reproduce; "otherwise . . . the race of such workmen could not last beyond the first generation."

Not only does a thriving society tend to raise wages; it tends to increase the rent received by the landlord. But there is not this correlation between the private interests of the capitalist and the common prosperity of society. Consequently, in considering the regulation of commerce, it is important to remember that of "the three great, original, and constituent orders of every civilized society"—those that live by wages, those that live by rent, and those that live by profits—the advice of the third class is suspect. "It comes from an order of men whose interest is never exactly the same with that of the public, who have generally an interest to deceive and even to oppress the public, and who accordingly have, upon many occasions, both deceived and oppressed it." [79]

Nevertheless, it is this peculiarly dangerous class that activates the economic system, that seeks investment for its superfluous capital, and that thereby creates a demand for labor and a demand for land, for which respectively it is ready and willing to pay wages and rent. For if a man possess capital, he will either consume it, invest it in fixed capital like machines, or invest in circulating capital like a payroll to operate the machines. "A man must be perfectly crazy who, where there is tolerable security, does not employ all the stock which he commands, whether it be his own or borrowed of other people, in some one or other of those three ways." [80] It is the task of government to supply the security.

It is not the task of government, however, to meddle with the economic system in order to "encourage" this or that activity; labor, land, and capital naturally come to market, when needed, by the natural law of supply and demand. But government has interfered with that process, because a false political economy has assumed that the wealth of a nation consists in a surplus of money. Hence government assists industry and particularly favors all forms of export trade, since they will bring in money. But money is not revenue: money is "the great wheel of circulation, the great instrument of commerce," [81] and wherever commerce flourishes, money will inevitably be drawn to that place.

The object of political economy, says Smith, is "to enrich both the people and the sovereign." Two chief systems of political economy have been proposed: the commercial, or mercantile, system and the agricultural system made famous in France by the group known as "the Economists." Although Smith finds exaggeration and paradox in the agricultural system, he finds in it also a wholesome deliverance from the monopolies, tariffs, bounties, embargoes, and navigation acts of the mercantile system afflicting England. The mercantile system completely reversed the traditional hierarchy of occupations. Smith agrees with the medieval order: agriculture, manufacture, trade. But the mercantilists placed trade first, particularly foreign trade; manufacture second; and agriculture they neglected and op-

pressed. Even the great Locke had sinned by supposing that national wealth consisted in increasing the
nation's supply of gold and silver. And these tariffs
and embargoes, which monopoly-mad tradesmen
persuade government to accord them, maintain for
them a "monopoly of the home market, . . . a
monopoly against their countrymen." [82] Smith finds
tariffs or embargoes excusable only when some industry is necessary for defense, or to compensate for a
domestic tax. In the second case, if a given article
is taxed when produced at home, a tariff imposing
an equal tax on the same article when made elsewhere and imported would merely in effect place
them back on a footing of even competition, a situation which from Smith's point of view is always desirable.

But the first case is different. Here, the "natural"
law of supply and demand, which allows goods and
services to flow where most wanted, is "violently"
interfered with in order that the state may be better
prepared in the event of that worse violence called
war. The act of navigation is a case in point: it
penalized the carrying trade of the Dutch, as well as
the pocketbook of the consumer, in order to build
up the carrying trade of Britain against a possible
naval war. "As defence . . . is of much more importance than opulence, the act of navigation is,
perhaps, the wisest of all the commercial regulations
of England." [83]

This sanction of present economic violence in the
interest of possible future political violence is inter-
esting, since Smith does not even suggest the alter-
natives: an enlargement of the political state based

on "natural" political rights that would make it safe
to leave intact all man's "natural" economic rights.
Smith is completely aware that the Union of England
and Scotland had been of enormous advantage in
admitting more men to citizenship in the Market-
place. His cure for "the present disturbances" in
America (*The Wealth of Nations,* was published,
remember, in 1776) was to invite the American
colonies to union with Britain, giving them pro-
portional representation in Parliament and equal
economic rights, instead of oppressing them with
legislation that for the most part enriched not
Britain, but a handful of British monopolists with
the ear of the Crown and Parliament. In the year
the book appeared, Britain's American colonies re-
volted; and eleven years after that, their delegates
assembled at Philadelphia and created there what
would one day become a far more spacious Market-
place than England and Scotland put together. Perhaps it is needless to add that Smith did not suggest
as even theoretically desirable a federation of politically free communities to secure the economic freedom of the Great Mercantile Republic, the republic
of all those men who trucked, bartered, and ex-
changed commodities with one another. Yet his
defense of the Act of Navigation shows how violence
breeds violence, and it shows that already the
existing political states were no longer extensive
enough to secure the commerce of peoples.

For most of the governmental regulations he has
nothing but scorn: "The laudable motives of all
these regulations is to extend our own manufactures,
not by their own improvement, but by the depres-

sion of those of all our neighbours, and by putting an end, as much as possible, to the troublesome competition of such odious and disagreeable rivals." [84] And again: "It cannot be very difficult to determine who have been the contrivers of this whole mercantile system; not the consumers, we may believe, whose interest has been entirely neglected; but the producers, whose interest has been so carefully attended to; and among this latter class our merchants and manufacturers have been by far the principal architects." [85]

Smith thought very little of businessmen in government, and very little of swapping tariff reductions with other countries. "The sneaking arts of underling tradesmen are thus erected into political maxims for the conduct of a great empire: for it is the most underling tradesmen only who make it a rule to employ chiefly their own customers. A great trader purchases his goods always where they are cheapest and best, without regard to any little interest of this kind.

"By such maxims as these, however, nations have been taught that their interest consisted in beggaring all their neighbours. Each nation has been made to look with an invidious eye upon the prosperity of all the nations with which it trades, and to consider their gain as its own loss. Commerce, which ought naturally to be, among nations, as among individuals, a bond of union and friendship, has become the most fertile source of discord and animosity. The capricious ambition of kings and ministers has not, during the present and the preceding century, been more fatal to the repose of Europe than the impertinent jealousy of merchants and manufacturers. The violence and injustice of the rulers of mankind is an ancient evil, for which, I am afraid, the nature of human affairs can scarce admit of a remedy. But the mean rapacity, the monopolising spirit of merchants and manufacturers, who neither are, nor ought to be, the rulers of mankind, though it cannot perhaps be corrected may very easily be prevented from disturbing the tranquillity of anybody but themselves.

"That it was the spirit of monopoly which originally both invented and propagated this doctrine cannot be doubted; and they who first taught it were by no means such fools as they who believed it." [86]

On the subject of colonies, Smith points out in the same vein that the same mean rapacity and monopolizing spirit have made the American colonies and British India a source of profit to private interests like the East India Company and a financial burden to the British people. Yet the discovery of America and the discovery of the route around Africa "are the two greatest and most important events recorded in the history of mankind," since both America and India threw a mass of commodities "into the great circle of European commerce."

For the mercantile system, with its meddling monopolies that clotted the circulatory system of commerce, and for the agricultural system with its extravagant claims for agriculture at the expense of the subsidiary but necessary activities, industry and commerce, Smith would substitute a minimum of government intervention in the natural human process of purchase and sale. Hobbes and Locke and Rousseau demanded that religion, at least in its institutionalized form of a church, should not be allowed to interfere with politics. Smith now urges that political authority refrain from interfering in the economic process, or at least that such interference be minimal. We shall recall that freed of that interference, the individual, with his natural propensity to truck, barter, and exchange, is "led by an invisible hand to promote an end which was no part of his intention. . . . By pursuing his own interest he frequently promotes that of the society more effectually than when he really intends to promote it. I have never known much good done by those who affected to trade for the public good. It is an affectation, indeed, not very common among merchants, and very few words need be employed in dissuading them from it." [87]

If, with Ruskin, we accuse Smith of positing individual love of gain as the surest route to the common good, let us remember his contempt for the greed of monopoly, as exhibited in some of the passages just quoted. Smith is tired of watching consumers milked by a monopolistic greed that mumbles the catch phrase, "the common good." And he believes he has demonstrated that in the economic area, as in the political area, the common good is best served by freedom. If the religious freedom, Smith might ask, that permits men to worship in their own fashion, is a good thing; if the freedom of speech, that lets them say what they think, is good; why is it sordid to let them buy or sell as each may choose? If a man has a house to sell, is he unjust to want "the market price"? And is not that the best price the house will fetch at this time and in this place? There is nothing in *The Wealth of Nations* to prevent his donating the proceeds to the poor. But why should he confuse sale and donation. Recall Smith's assumption that commerce "ought naturally to be, among nations, as among individuals, a bond of union and friendship . . ." It is this union and friendship that bind together the buying and selling citizens of the Market-place.

The sovereign, who presides over the Market-place, clarifies its economic dialectic by providing for it the medium of money; minimizes deception and economic sophistry by providing true weights and measures; protects the buying-and-selling dialectic likewise from violence, even—as far as possible—from the violence of monopoly. The sovereign therefore has three real functions, as distinguished from the meddling that mercantilism had authorized: defense; internal justice; and those public works and public institutions which are of economic benefit to society but which no private citizen or group of citizens would have the economic resources to undertake. Beyond those three functions it cannot help, though it may often hurt, the Market-place.

It is essentially in Adam Smith's Market-place in his Great Mercantile Republic, that John Stuart Mill sets up his ethics (in *Utilitarianism*) and his politics (in his essays *On Liberty* and *Representative Government*). He brings to his task the same appeal to common experience, the same keen observation, the

same salty wit, as his British predecessors Hobbes
and Locke and Smith. He soars no farther than they
into metaphysical speculation.

The foundation of morality, says Mill, is "Utility,
or the Greatest Happiness Principle." [88] He agrees
with Aristotle, on the simple basis of observation,
that what all men seek is happiness; but he insists on
defining happiness as quite simply the acquisition
of pleasures and the avoidance of pain. He foresees
the charge that this is the way a swine would look
at happiness, and replies quietly that swinish pleasures do not satisfy human beings. Man aims higher
for his pleasures and willingly suffers more to obtain them. "It is better to be a human being dissatisfied than a pig satisfied; better to be Socrates
dissatisfied than a fool satisfied. And if the fool, or
the pig, are of a different opinion, it is because
they only know their own side of the question. The
other party to the comparison knows both sides." [89]

Mill shares the cheerfulness of his generation
about the amount of human happiness that is obtainable on this earth, and thinks that "no one whose
opinion deserves a moment's consideration can
doubt that most of the great positive evils of the
world are in themselves removable, and will, if
human affairs continue to improve, be in the end
reduced within narrow limits." [90] The only meaning Mill can find in Kant's categorical imperative is
"that we ought to shape our conduct by a rule which
all rational beings might adopt *with benefit to their
collective interest.*" [91] To the charge that Utility is
an uncertain standard of human behavior compared
with "the immutable, ineffaceable, and unmistak-

able dictates of Justice" [92] he has little difficulty in pointing out that both principles are abstractly clear and that the application of either to concrete cases leads to a great variety of opinions.

For man to seek his happiness effectually, Mill, like Locke, wants man free; but whereas Locke is busy freeing man from Hobbes's "Sovereign" and permitting him and his fellows to live under reasonable laws made by majority rule, Mill in his essay *On Liberty,* goes further and wants to free him from the tyranny of the majority. He will not, like Rousseau, look for any kind of liberty through losing one's will in the general will: he states flatly that "liberty consists in doing what one desires," and he wants to find "the nature and limits of the power which can be legitimately exercised by society over the individual" either by the state through law or by one's neighbors through social pressure. He finds it in "one very simple principle, as entitled to govern absolutely the dealings of society with the individual in the way of compulsion and control, whether the means used be physical force in the form of legal penalties, or the moral coercion of public opinion. That principle is, that the sole end for which mankind are warranted, individually or collectively, in interfering with the liberty of action of any of their number is self-protection. . . . His own good, either physical or moral, is not a sufficient warrant." [93] Again: "The only freedom which deserves the name, is that of pursuing our own good in our own way, so long as we do not attempt to deprive others of theirs, or impede their efforts to obtain it." [94]

So far, Mill has given us the sturdy, independent

if not stubborn, "natural" man whom Hobbes feared as an anarchist, whom Locke defended against tyranny: that, plus an awareness of the social tyranny that may wither freedom even in Locke's ideal state. But, when Mill discusses specifically "the liberty of thought and discussion," there is an echo of his hero Socrates and of the noble uses of dialectic. Freedom of speech is necessary to come at the truth. He gives the authoritarian case against such freedom, together with his answer:

"Men, and governments, must act to the best of their ability. There is no such thing as absolute certainty, but there is assurance sufficient for the purposes of human life. We may, and must, assume our opinion to be true for the guidance of our own conduct: and it is assuming no more when we forbid bad men to pervert society by the propagation of opinions which we regard as false and pernicious.

"I answer, that it is assuming very much more. There is the greatest difference between presuming an opinion to be true, because, with every opportunity for contesting it, it has not been refuted, and assuming its truth for the purpose of not permitting its refutation. Complete liberty of contradicting and disproving our opinion is the very condition which justifies us in assuming its truth for purposes of action; and on no other terms can a being with human faculties have any rational assurance of being right." [95] This is a clearer statement for toleration than either Milton or Locke made. Nor will Mill except those doctrines which, while not true, are socially useful. Against that new claim for censorship, Mill parries swiftly: "The usefulness of an opinion is itself matter of opinion: as disputable, as open to discussion, and requiring discussion as much as the opinion itself." [96] And Socratically he holds that "No one can be a great thinker who does not recognise, that as a thinker it is his first duty to follow his intellect to whatever conclusions it may lead." [97]

So much for the attempt to protect from discussion an opinion that may happen to be false. But even on the hypothesis that it is actually true, it needs dialectical examination, the clash of opposite opinion: "However true it may be, if it is not fully, frequently, and fearlessly discussed, it will be held as a dead dogma, not a living truth. . . .[98] Truth, thus held, is but one superstition the more, accidentally clinging to the words which enunciate a truth. . . .[99] He who knows only his own side of the case, knows little of that. . . .[100] The fatal tendency of mankind to leave off thinking about a thing when it is no longer doubtful, is the cause of half their errors. A contemporary author has spoken well of 'the deep slumber of a decided opinion.' " [101] We need the "Socratic dialectics, so magnificently exemplified in the dialogues of Plato," [102] or even the "school disputations of the Middle Ages." [103] Mill thinks "the modern mind owes far more to both than it is generally willing to admit, and the present modes of education contain nothing which in the smallest degree supplies the place either of the one or of the other." [104]

Noting the dead and deadly weight of mass opinion in the Market-place that the City of Man has become, Mill urges deliberate revolt: "that exceptional individuals, instead of being deterred, should be encouraged in acting differently from the mass. In other times there was no advantage in their doing so, unless they acted not only differently but better. In this age, the mere example of non-conformity, the mere refusal to bend the knee to custom, is itself a service. Precisely because the tyranny of opinion is such as to make eccentricity a reproach, it is desirable, in order to break through that tyranny, that people should be eccentric. . . . That so few now dare to be eccentric marks the chief danger of the time." [105]

Mill fully shares Adam Smith's distrust of paternalistic government, and his essay *On Liberty* ends with the words: "The worth of a State, in the long run, is the worth of the individuals composing it; and a State which postpones the interest of *their* mental expansion and elevation to a little more of administrative skill, or of that semblance of it which practice gives, in the details of business; a State which dwarfs its men, in order that they may be made more docile instruments in its hands even for beneficial purposes—will find that with small men no great thing can really be accomplished; and that the perfection of machinery to which it has sacrificed everything will in the end avail it nothing, for want of the vital power which, in order that the machine might work more smoothly, it has preferred to banish." [106]

In *Representative Government* Mill holds that the best kind of government, ideally, is popular government, both because it furnishes better government immediately and because it promotes a better and higher form of national character than any other form can. It governs better immediately, partly because men stand up for their own rights and interests better than other people stand up for them and partly because, as Adam Smith so clearly saw, those communities thrive most in which the maximum number of men throw their energies into the social enterprise. This plea for enlarging the suffrage sounds like an argument by a liberal of today until Mill coolly lays down some qualifications that few liberals of today would tolerate. He holds that "universal teaching must precede universal enfranchisement";[107] that a poll tax is an excellent method of guaranteeing that nobody except those who contribute to the common treasury shall have the power to spend from it; that, for the same reason, those on relief cannot possibly expect to vote. Far from exhorting people to go to the polls, he does not wish voting made easy for those who are indifferent to the privilege: "A man who does not care whether he votes, is not likely to care much which way he votes; and he who is in that state of mind has no moral right to vote at all; since, if he does so, a vote which is not the expression of a conviction, counts for as much, and goes as far in determining the result, as one which represents the thoughts and purposes of a life." [108] He would presumably have loathed the American election-eve cliché that the Presidency of the United States is "the highest office in the gift of the American people." For he declares: "There is scarcely any mode in which political institutions are more morally mischievous—work greater evil through their spirit—than by representing political functions as a favor to be conferred, . . ." [109] He is opposed to the secret ballot, because he believes it leads voters to think of the ballot as a private benefit and not a public trust. There is an echo of Rousseau and Kant in his declaration that the ballot "has no more to do with his personal wishes than the verdict of a juryman. It is strictly a matter of duty; he is bound to give it according to his best and most conscientious opinion of the public good. Whoever has any other idea of it is unfit to have the suffrage; . . ." [110]

It will be observed that one strain runs through the passages just quoted. In the ideal society everybody ought to participate in government, but it is as necessary that the sovereign act responsibly and rationally where it is the people as where it is a monarch. Mill would never have written the title to one of our documentary films during the Second World War: "It's Fun to Be Free." On the contrary, he looked on freedom as a difficult duty, to which all men should be called who can possibly be expected to fulfill it. In "democracy," as praised today, he would have found no such rigor, and no such challenge.

Mill's understanding of "federal representative government" goes far beyond those first indistinct insights of men like Locke and Rousseau, or even Montesquieu. On this subject he is worth quoting at length:

"There are two different modes of organising a Federal Union. The federal authorities may represent the Governments solely, and their acts may be obligatory only on the Governments as such; or they may have the power of enacting laws and issuing orders which are binding directly on individual citizens. The former is the plan of the German so-called Confederation, and of the Swiss Constitution previous to 1847. It was tried in America for a few years immediately following the War of Independence. The other principle is that of the existing Constitution of the United States, and has been adopted within the last dozen years by the Swiss Confederacy. The Federal Congress of the American Union is a substantive part of the government of every individual State. Within the limits of its attributions, it makes laws which are obeyed by every citizen individually, executes them through its own officers, and enforces them by its own tribunals. This is the only principle which has been found, or which is ever likely, to produce an effective federal government. A union between the governments only is a mere alliance, and subject to all the contingencies which render alliances precarious. If the acts of the President and of Congress were binding solely on the Governments of New York, Virginia, or Pennsylvania, and could only be carried into effect through orders issued by those Governments to officers appointed by them, under responsibility to their own courts of justice, no mandates of the Federal Government which were disagreeable to a local majority would ever be executed. Requisitions issued to a government have no other sanction, or means of enforcement, than war: and a federal army would have to be always in readiness to enforce the decrees of the Federation against any recalcitrant State; subject to the probability that other States, sympathising with the recusant, and perhaps sharing its sentiments on the particular point in dispute, would withhold their contingents, if not send them to fight in the ranks of the disobedient State. Such a federation is more likely to be a cause than a preventive of internal wars: and if such was not its effect in Switzerland until the events of the years immediately preceding 1847, it was only because the Federal Government felt its weakness so strongly that it hardly ever attempted to exercise any real authority. In America, the experiment of a Federation on this principle broke down in the first few years of its existence; happily while the men of enlarged knowledge and acquired ascendancy, who founded the independence of the Republic, were still alive to guide it through the difficult transition. The *Federalist,* a collection of papers by three of these eminent men, written in explanation and defence of the new Federal Constitution while still awaiting the national acceptance, is even now the most instructive treatise we possess on federal government. . . . When the conditions exist for the formation of efficient and durable Federal Unions, the multiplication of them is always a benefit to the world." [111]

Where Mill saw in Adam Smith's Market-place not only the free competition of commodities but the nobler free competition of ideas, the German philosopher Hegel saw in the history of mankind and in the history of his own national state a dialectical motion from one social embodiment of the Divine Idea to a counter-embodiment; then a conflict between this "thesis" and its "antithesis," finally resolving itself in a synthesis.

For Hegel's Divine Idea, working itself out dialectically, his self-declared disciple Karl Marx saw a society politically organized by and in favor of a new economic class which had recently seized the economic means of production. But he agrees with Hegel that history does in fact advance "dialectically" through successive systems that are thesis, antithesis, synthesis. The dialectic, however, is not governed by Hegel's "final cause . . . the *consciousness* of its own freedom on the part of Spirit." Indeed, in Aristotle's terms, it is not governed by any final cause at all, but by a material cause: the economic structure of society, the sum total of the relations of production. And the dialectic is between economic classes. The latest stage of that dialectic is the stage which Marx calls Capitalism, a stage which he explores in his most famous work, *Capital (A Critique of Political Economy)*. Marx's collaborator Engels claimed in his Preface to the first English edition of *Capital* that it was often called, on the Continent, the Bible of the working class. Whether or not it has earned that title, it is certainly the Bible of the Communist, and this fact alone guarantees that it will be for our immediate time and place the most controversial book discussed in this essay. As so often happens with bibles, *Capital* has not been carefully read by most persons, including the faithful; it is long and in spots technical. Yet it is so brilliantly and persuasively written that its major concepts have permeated the whole of contemporary thought. And it is by no means unusual to hear those concepts unconsciously employed by those who would like to see Marx's works strictly banned and all Communists shot! It is these persons, particularly, who ought to study *Capital* most assiduously, in order to understand better the concepts they assiduously and unwittingly use.

Probably more readers would discover this profoundly analytical book, had they not been nauseated by the habit of many Marxists of turning Marx's analysis into half-understood dogmas and catchphrases in order to exempt themselves from the pain of thinking. In the same fashion, more readers would discover the profoundly analytical writings of Thomas Aquinas, had they not been nauseated by the habit of many Thomists of turning Thomas's analysis into half-understood dogmas and catchphrases in order to exempt themselves, also, from the pain of thinking. But the pain of thinking is a pain which, if dodged by many Marxists and many Thomists, both Marx and Thomas bravely faced. That we have all been a little deafened by Marxist clamor should not prevent us from listening intently to what Marx himself said. That we have all been a little bored by his fanatical followers should not prevent us from listening to a book that is one of the least boring ever written.

It is not Marx's achievement to tell us that the rich oppress the poor. The Bible will do that. Plato will tell us of the two cities that "the City" usually contains: the rich and the poor. Thomas will declare that the Christian should not even lend money at interest. Rousseau will tell us that "laws are always of use to those who possess and harmful to those who have nothing: from which it follows that the social state is advantageous to men only when all have something and none too much." [112] Even Adam Smith, who extolled the accumulation of "stock," or of what we now call "capital," knew well that the interests of the wage-earner and the interest of the employer "are by no means the same." And although Smith trusted to the "natural" law of supply and demand, to competition in all areas, and to a "thriving," or expanding, economy to furnish the wage-earner with something better than bare subsistence; yet he was only too aware of the genius of the capitalist for monopoly, and his habit of securing it either by persuading the government to intervene on his behalf or by conspiring secretly against the laws that forbade monopoly. In Smith's picture of the Market-place the capitalist is not a pretty fellow, though "an invisible hand," aided by a vigilant umpire-government, makes the self-interest of even the capitalist serve the common good of the Market-place.

Nor is it Marx's achievement to derive all economic "value" from labor. So did Hobbes and Locke and Smith and Mill. What Marx did was to analyze in detail the actual operation of an essentially new economic system, the capitalist system of production and distribution in the throes of industrialization, and to argue that we live, neither in a City of God governed by God, nor in a City of Man governed by the natural laws and human reason which God made, but in a Market-place governed by force and deception, and destined to an early collapse. He is therefore a prophet of doom. But he is also a prophet of hope. For out of this inevitable and indeed desirable collapse of the Market-place will emerge a new City, a City of economic as well as political freedom, whose fore-ordained citizens will be all men everywhere who eat their bread by the sweat of their face.

Capital first offers a full analysis of commodities, and how money measures their "value"—that is, their exchange-value. For even air has a "use-value." As values, says *Capital,* "commodities are mere congelations of human labour, . . ." [113] It is man-hours of human labor that convert natural resources into commodities. Marx quotes Benjamin Franklin on this point: "Trade in general being nothing else than the exchange of labour for labour, the value of all things is . . . most justly measured by labour." [114] Even money, Marx insists, is not merely a symbol but a commodity: it, too, is congealed labor-time. For it takes labor to mine gold and silver: hard cash is merely "value petrified." Most of this, although stated with a mastery of metaphor worthy of Hobbes, is relatively orthodox economics —or as Marx would say, "bourgeois" economics, the economic thinking of the capitalist class.

Marx's originality comes into play at the point where money is converted into "capital." To accomplish this feat, says Marx, the money must be converted into some commodity capable of itself creating value, and this commodity is "labour power": man-hours for sale, if you like. You cannot turn money into capital merely by buying a commodity which has been made by a worker to sell; for the maker-seller will demand its full value. He will then be offering his own labor-time against the labor-time incorporated in the money price—or in the commodity which once fetched that money price. The trick of capitalism is to offer less in wages—the less, the better—than the product, that these wages will cause the worker to produce, can be sold for. At that point we "take leave for a time of this noisy sphere where everything takes place on the surface and in view of all men, and follow them both [the capitalist and the labourer] into the hidden abode of production, on whose threshold there stares us in the face: 'No admittance except on business.' Here we shall see, not only how capital produces, but how capital is produced. We shall at last force the secret of profit making.

"This sphere that we are deserting, within whose boundaries the sale and purchase of labour power goes on, is in fact a very Eden of the innate rights of man. There alone rule freedom, equality, property and Bentham [an early exponent of Mill's doctrine of Utilitarianism]. Freedom, because both buyer and seller of a commodity, say a labour power, are constrained only by their own free will. They contract as free agents, and the agreement they come to is but the form in which they give legal expression to their common will. Equality, because each enters into relation with the other, as with a simple owner of commodities, and they exchange equivalent for equivalent. Property, because each disposes only of what is his own. And Bentham, because each looks only to himself. The only force that brings them together and puts them in relation with each other, is the selfishness, the gain, and the private interests of each. Each looks to himself only, and no one troubles himself about the rest; and just because they do so, do they all, in accordance with the pre-established harmony of things, or under the auspices of an all-wise providence, work together for their mutual advantage, for the common weal, and in the interest of all.

"On leaving this sphere of simple circulation or of exchange of commodities, which furnishes the Free-trader *Vulgaris* with his views and ideas, and with the standard by which he judges a society based on capital and wages, we think we can perceive a change in the physiognomy of our *dramatis personae*. He, who before was the money owner, now strides in front as capitalist; the possessor of labour power follows as his labourer. The one with an air of importance, smirking, intent on business; the other, timid and holding back, like one who is bringing his own hide to market and has nothing to expect but—a hiding." [115]

In that hidden abode, to which there is no admittance except on business, Marx is confident he beheld a gruesome thing happen: the capitalist "extracted" from the worker, as if by a surgical operation, a "surplus value." This consists in the difference between the wage paid to the laborer, a wage which—Adam Smith to the contrary notwithstanding—has not always by any means allowed the laborer "to subsist and to reproduce," and this laborer's share of the saleable output of the hidden abode. This is the "profit," which becomes new capital to build new hidden abodes with, and to employ more workers from whom to extract more surplus value. This is why Marx promised to show us, inside the abode, "not only how capital produces, but how capital is produced."

The Industrial Revolution, with its vast machines and its mass production, was just beginning when Smith wrote, and Adam Smith had based his economic theory largely on handicraft production. But Marx is looking at factories and machines. He is also looking at a huge reservoir of "free" labor: men, women, and children, driven off the land that had through their toil supported them. Sometimes this had been done by illegal means; sometimes a Parliament, which was dominated by labor-hungry capitalists, had done it by laws. This half-starved proletariat was available at starvation wages. Men, women, and little children, they were escorted by the new class of factory-owners into the owners' "hidden abodes," where things happened to them that form one of the ugliest chapters in human history. Carefully documenting his statements from the reports of Parliamentary commissions, Karl Marx reports what those things were. He reports them indignantly, as Rousseau reported indignantly the cases he, too, had witnessed of man's inhumanity to man. But Marx is careful to say that what we are witnessing in this Inferno of production and profit, this Inferno in which modern industrial society was forged, is not so much individual malefactors as a system of production: Capitalism. This system is a

Frankenstein's monster, which is devouring those who created it. The workers are helpless. In the face of competition those capitalists who would have preferred to be decent are forced into line. Superficially, these small children, working fifteen hours a day until exhaustion, disease, and death free them at last, are under the will of the overseer and his lash. But the overseer and even the owner are under the lash of Capital. Once men used tools; now tools, in the shape of machines of increasing size and velocity, use men—use them and throw them away, as men once threw worn-out tools away.

Faced with this horror, faced with the lesser but still great horror of the means the capitalist class had used to get the poor at their mercy even before the day of Adam Smith, Marx is bitterly scornful of Smith's idyllic picture of free men selling commodities to each other in a free Market-place, governed by "an invisible hand" that mysteriously converted individual self-interest into the common weal. But he applauded Smith for perceiving the importance of the division of labor. It was this division of labor that brought laborers together, increased their output, and through a ghastly discipline taught them the necessity of wresting from the capitalist some day the machines that enslaved them to their hurt, and taught them also the necessity of enslaving those machines to the worker. In the political area the Hobbesian Sovereign may have tyrannized, but he socialized too: he brought men up out of anarchy into tyranny. Rousseau could then tell the Sovereign's subjects that the state belonged to them, not to their tyrant. Now, in the economic area the Marxian Capitalist had brought the laboring class up out of the land of handicraft and low production, first into that division of labor that so greatly increased output, and now into the complex organization of machine production. That new organization was a fearful economic tyranny, but Marx views it as a necessary stage. For the whole tendency of the capitalist system, as he observes it, is towards greater and greater monopoly: big capitalists force little capitalists to the wall. As the ownership of society's means of production comes to be concentrated in fewer and fewer hands, the opportunity for the working class to expropriate those means also increases —as the capitalists had once expropriated the land of the working class in order to secure "free" laborers from whom to extract surplus value. Meanwhile, the recurrent economic crises of "over-production" and unemployment will drive the wretched workers into worldwide combination against their tormentor —not a machine nor a capitalist, but the capitalist system itself, the system that forces both the capitalist and the machine to behave the way they behave.

Marx attempts to show how inexorably this system grows, like some devouring monster. It destroys the skilled craftsman who knows what he is doing and why; and it replaces him with "labor power," or converts him into "labor power" himself, into a wage-slave who is a slave precisely because he is under compulsion to do what he is told whether he understands it or not. The division of labor now becomes a curse, and it colors the whole of society.

Smith had reveled in the fact that the increased efficiency of the division of labor applied even to the intellectual labor of the scholar. But Marx observes that, as more and more men are assigned petty tasks in every sphere without understanding why they are to be done, the worker on every level becomes that much less a man. And he quotes Adam Smith's own teacher Ferguson who could exclaim decades before machine production had exaggerated the division of labor: "We make a nation of helots and have no free citizens." [116] Marx saw that the factory system of capitalism, by pressing down wages, lengthening work hours, and speeding up machinery wherever possible, in order to increase surplus value and thereby speed the accumulation of capital, not only offered the workman insecurity, fatigue, hunger, cold, filth, disease, and social degradation; it also reduced him from craftsman to automaton. "While simple cooperation leaves the mode of working by the individual for the most part unchanged, manufacture thoroughly revolutionises it and seizes labour power by its very roots. It converts the labourer into a crippled monstrosity, by forcing his detail dexterity at the expense of a world of productive capabilities and instincts; just as in Argentina they butcher a whole beast for the sake of his hide or his tallow. Not only is the detail work distributed to the different individuals, but the individual himself is made the automatic motor of a fractional operation, and the absurd fable of Menenius Agrippa, which makes man a mere fragment of his own body, becomes realized. . . . By nature unfitted to make anything independently, the manufacturing labourer develops productive activity as a mere appendage of the capitalist's workshop. As the chosen people bore in their features the sign manual of Jehovah, so division of labour brands the manufacturing workman as the property of capital." [117] But this crippled monster, this over-specialized, and hence dulled and frustrated, urban proletarian, in his slum dwelling will develop a certain kind of deadly efficiency, for as Adam Smith had observed long ago, "a man commonly saunters a little in changing occupations." The single, fragmentary, and hence (to the worker) meaningless task will soon take this saunter out of man.

In addition to reducing a class of craftsmen, who are whole men, into a class of robots, who are half-men, machinery greatly increases the opportunity for surplus value, and thereby greatly increases the accumulation and concentration of capital. Its method of doing this is simple. By vastly increasing output, it lessens the fraction of a day's work that must pay the worker's subsistence wage, and increases the ratio pocketed as profit: the surplus value. In his *Principles of Political Economy* Mill had written: "It is questionable if all the mechanical inventions yet made have lightened the day's toil of any human being." [118] But, says Marx bitterly, that is not the point of labor-saving devices. The point is "to cheapen commodities and, by shortening that portion of the working day, in which the labourer works for himself, to lengthen the other portion that he gives without an equivalent to the capitalist. In short, it is a means for producing surplus value." [119]

As machine production matures, it becomes of necessity co-operative, "social." Because machines are capitalist-owned and directed to capitalist accumulation, their first social effects are destructive. They call women and children as well as men—and sometimes, quite deliberately, instead of men—into the factory, thereby converting the father of the family from a wage-slave to a slave trader. They tend to lengthen, not shorten, the working day, precisely by dangling a greater profit before the capitalist. They intensify the working day for the same reason. And they furnish a constant weapon in the hands of the capitalist, who can always threaten the recalcitrant worker with being replaced by machinery.

Nevertheless, by substituting factory production and factory economy for domestic economy, they lay the economic foundation for a new kind of family life; for, says Marx, there is nothing sacrosanct about the "home life" of a given era, itself merely the expression of transient means of production. Modern production has become "social." This will be the basis for the classless society of the future, when the capitalist has been expropriated by the present working class. The capitalist class will have fulfilled its historic role and been destroyed—as the feudal nobility had once fulfilled its own mission and had been destroyed by the capitalist class!

Adam Smith, in positing his economic trinity of labor, stock, and rent, had assumed that the stock, or capital, came originally from "previous accumulation" through labor: the ultimate source of all value. But Marx points out, with abundant documentation, where this previous, or "primary," accumulation came from—in short, where the capitalist got hold of his first capital. He got it by seizing the worker's means of production, and the theft took a long historical period to consummate. It involved the expropriation of peasant lands, the famous Parliamentary acts of "enclosure," and "the clearing of estates" of workers' cottages, thereby driving them to the new labor-hungry, industrial towns. The process created a new class: the laboring poor as they were called in England, as distinguished from the idle poor. These were the wage-earners. They were no longer feudally bound to the land, nor was the land bound to them. They were bound to nothing. They were propertyless, except for the "labor power" in their bodies. Given this history, Marx is acid about those capitalists and their hireling political economists who mistake for "natural laws" the customs of the economic era—the capitalist era —in which they happen to live and thrive. He scornfully quotes Edmund Burke: "The laws of commerce are the laws of Nature, and therefore the laws of God." "No wonder," Marx retorts, "that, true to the laws of God and Nature, he always sold himself in the best market." [120]

How accidental these laws of God and Nature are, Marx shows by pointing to the colonies, where "the working poor" had a chance to choose between working for a wage or annexing some free land and getting the full product of their labor. He quotes H. Merivale, an Oxford professor of political economy, as noting that in the colonies there is an "urgent desire for cheaper and more subservient labourers

—for a class to whom the capitalist might dictate terms, instead of being dictated to by them. . . . In ancient civilized countries, the labourer, though free, is by law of nature dependent on capitalists; in colonies this dependence must be created by artificial means." [121] This kind of law of nature is certainly not the one Rousseau appealed to when he discussed social contracts. Marx himself observes drily that only in the colonies there exist the "men and conditions that could turn a social contract from a dream to a reality." [122]

But where Rousseau hated and feared money and the power of the rich, Marx accepted them, not with Merivale of Oxford as dictated by natural law, but as part of the long dialectic of history in which successive economic systems had by their oppression called forth their respective negations, their Hegelian "antitheses," only to give way to new syntheses, which themselves would necessarily call forth new antitheses to destroy them. These successive dialectical steps, represented historically by the revolt of economic groups in the long class struggle that Marxian history essentially is, culminate in the struggle between the capitalist class and the new proletariat which it created in order to exploit. Meanwhile, the capitalist class, the "bourgeoisie," in order to accumulate capital, will increase the means of social production on a machine basis; concentrate those means in fewer and fewer monopolistic hands; make over society in its own image, with its religious beliefs, its political and legal institutions, its esthetic values, its precious "natural" and eternal laws; and be swept away by proletarian revolt—the last revolt, Marx holds, for no exploited class remains to revolt in its turn, as always hitherto. It is the production of man's material necessities that determines all his values, as one system of pro duction follows another system. Capitalism is no exception. For "capital is not a thing, but a social relation between persons, and a relation determined by things." This definition of capital reminds us of Thomas Hobbes' definition of money as power over other men's labor.

So much talk about "will" in the City of Man: the "General Will"; the particular wills of men in Locke's state of Nature; Kant's categorical imperative, legislating universally; the wills of Hegel's world-historical persons; the almost divine will of Hegel's State, itself the Divine Idea as it exists on Earth; Adam Smith's multitude of particular human wills, looking to their own interest in the Marketplace, guided by an invisible hand to achieve the common good!

But the will of the individual, says Marx, means little. Events are determined in history by the great, dialectical class struggle, a struggle not merely of ideas or even of words, but of weapons, a struggle in which heads get broken. Man the reasoner, man the worshiper, man the lawmaker, man the buyer and seller. And now, man the worker, all but broken on the flywheel of the machine, stretched taut like Prometheus, his very vitals fed on by that hungry vulture, Capital.

Prometheus will yet be unbound. If *Capital* analyzes his inevitable torment with only an occasional angry tear for his pain, *The Communist Manifesto* offers him opportunity to merge his will with the will of inexorable History and win a final freedom. Men have spoken, prayed, made laws, trucked and bartered—but only because other men have worked —their own share and the share of those others. When the City of the Worker has been founded by the revolt of the wage-earner against Capital, no man need be oppressed, whether by philosophic absolute, or by God, or by the laws the exploiting class has always made, or by the moneychanger and merchant. All the long story of oppression, whether of noble, priest, or merchant, is unworthy of the name of history. It is pre-history. Only with the ending of these interminable class struggles by the final victory of the working class will true history begin!

And so, in *The Communist Manifesto,* Marx hurls his defiance at the bourgeoisie, the exploiting class in our modern, capitalistic society. He relates their own revolutionary history. He explains how they have destroyed the medieval culture of Europe and reduced all things to money profit. He points out that their system of production condemns them to a series of vast economic crises, to perpetual change in methods of production, to constant imperialism in search of new markets, to a cosmopolitanism that mocks national patriotism, to recurrent "overproduction" in the midst of human need; and above all, to the appalling danger of a growing class of industrial workers, of proletarians, ever more class-conscious, ever more intolerably oppressed. He points out that the sporadic outbursts of these oppressed wage-earners is welding them into solidarity.

These last "have nothing of their own to secure and to fortify; their mission is to destroy all previous securities for, and insurance of, individual property.

"All previous historical movements were movements of minorities, or in the interest of minorities. The proletarian movement is the self-conscious, independent movement in the interest of the immense majority, . . . The advance of industry, whose revolutionary promoter is the bourgeoisie, replaces the isolation of the labourers, due to competition, by their revolutionary combination, due to association. The development of modern industry, therefore, cuts from under its feet the very foundation on which the bourgeoisie produces and appropriates products. What the bourgeoisie therefore produces, above all are its own grave-diggers. Its fall and the victory of the proletariat are equally inevitable." [123]

To the cry of the bourgeois that Marx and his Communism would destroy culture, freedom, law, religion, the family, Marx retorts that these things have already been destroyed for all but a few by the bourgeoisie itself; or in some cases are mere façades for bourgeois exploitation, façades in which the bourgeois himself does not really believe.

Then Marx lays down the program for the revolution in property relations which he regards as both inevitable and eminently desirable. He denounces rival Socialist parties for supposing that the working class can be freed from exploitation within the framework of bourgeois society and by means of bourgeois institutions. Nor can it be freed by its would-be benefactor. It must free itself—by its own revolutionary action—and its freedom spells doom for the whole set of customs and institutions which the bourgeois regards as external and right, and which Marx regards as the transitory expressions of a system of production already on the way to the limbo of discarded things. "The Communists . . . declare that their ends can be attained only by the forcible overthrow of all existing social conditions. Let the ruling classes tremble at a Communistic revolution. The proletarians have nothing to lose but their chains. They have a world to win.

"Working men of all countries, unite!" [124]

Into Locke's Garden of Eden, his idyllic state of Nature in which each man was free and owned property, had crept a serpent named tyranny. Salvation from that serpent lay in law and reason, in free government, and government that would guarantee both freedom and private property—and perhaps a chance for the propertyless to acquire property.

Into Rousseau's Garden of Eden had crept a serpent, also, but the serpent was private property itself, and from the serpent of private property had been spawned a whole brood of evil and tyrannous things that are all expressed in the words inequality and civilization. But salvation could be found in the general will of common men, banded together against oppression and living a simple life.

Marx, however, could find no Garden of Eden in the past. The Garden is in the future—in a classless society. He agrees with Rousseau that civilization is rotten and is characterized by inequality; but that is because it is bourgeois civilization, and the bourgeoisie has already performed its historic mission of concentrating production in social form, vastly increasing its powers, and calling into being a proletariat that must find bourgeois oppression intolerable and must therefore revolt. That revolt, however, will clear away all inequality, leaving man the worker, free, and united in useful production with his fellow-worker. Man will then enter a new City, a new promised land, of plenty and of justice. Meanwhile, that shining City's embryo is the Proletariat; and the oppressed Proletariat moves through the Free Market-place of Adam Smith and Mill, as the "pilgrim city" of Augustine—the City of God—once moved through a corrupt and dying Dialectical Republic. It is to that Pilgrim Proletarian City, not turning the other cheek but clenching the upraised fist, that Marx summons the "working men of all countries" to unite themselves. It is a City, he implies, that will sweep away the Market-place, or rather the numerous petty Market-places that men call sovereign states; and with the bourgeoisie, the last oppressors of mankind, laid low, it will usher in the dawn of true human history.

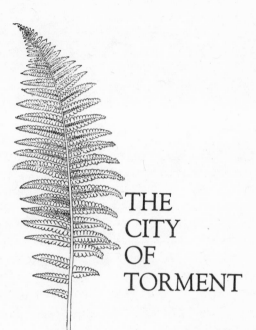

THE
CITY
OF
TORMENT

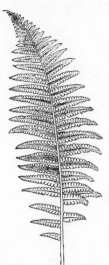

THE CITY OF TORMENT

Sigmund Freud looks to no such Eden —or Paradise. Man's tragedy, he finds, lies deeper than bourgeois exploitation, than economic oppression and poverty. It lies inside the soul, the psyche, and it preys on rich and poor alike. It is not poverty but madness that threatens man. He agrees with Marx in discarding religion and theology as nonsense; but where Marx found ultimate reality in economics, Freud found it in psychology. Deeper even than man's hunger for food, is man's sexual hunger. Out of that hunger, and not out of the organization of production, come all man's other achievements: his religious myths, his philosophy, his art, his techniques. The essence of man is not that he thinks, or prays, or legislates, or barters, or even that he works. The essence of man is that he loves, that he desires. Eros rules.

Freud was a doctor. His interests led him through brain anatomy to mental diseases. From watching the use of hypnosis to cure patients of obsessions, he came to discover that the cause of mental disorders was to be found in the deeper layers of the mind, in actions and events that were remembered unconsciously, not consciously. He discovered various means of getting at these hidden memories. By guiding his patient to talk haphazardly, by "free association," Freud could slowly uncover that patient's dreamlife, his fantasies, his forgotten early childhood. He discovered striking analogies between the dream and childhood, between both of these and primitive societies. And back of all of them he found the guiding principle of sexual desire.

Small wonder that the revolutionary psychologist Freud aroused as much hate, if not as much fear, as the revolutionary economist Marx. If the bourgeois preferred not to enter the hidden abode of Marx's capitalist production, he was even less willing to enter a hidden abode which turned out to be his own innermost self, an abode where things even less mentionable happened than happened in the factory. Nobody wants to discover "base" motives in himself—unless, like Freud, he questions the validity of the term base.

Everybody could find excuses for not looking. Freud, like Marx, denounced religion; the bourgeois would recoil sharply from that indecency, particularly since he was often not very religious himself, but ardently pretended to be. As to ethics, where Marx denounced bourgeois ethics as having only a temporary and declining significance, Freud looked on all ethics as society's not too successful attempt to curb the wild heart of man, and as therefore essentially oppressive. Where Marx declined to respect the state or the law which the bourgeois defended—and profited by—Freud felt melancholy misgivings about any law, bourgeois or Communist. Finally, where the devout Marxist often bored his friends by reducing everything he saw to capitalist oppression, the coming triumph of the proletariat, surplus value, class struggle, and a host of other terms, Freud let loose the seductive terminology of psychoanalysis: complexes, inhibitions, repressions, the ego and the id, the unconscious, libido, dream-work, and a multitude of others, which the faithful too often mumbled confusedly but ecstatically. But, as nobody has discovered a detour around the problems Marx raised, so nobody has discovered a detour around those raised by Freud. We are at liberty to seek other solutions to those problems, but we appear quite unable not to look at the phenomena at which Marx and Freud point. We are, of course, still trying not to.

It is possible to find Plato and Aristotle in Freud, as indeed it is possible to find Hobbes or Rousseau or Spinoza. But his unique genius lies in his courageous and systematic exploration of the hidden motives of the human heart: he does scientifically what perhaps only Dostoevsky does comparably in the field of poetic art. And as one follows Freud on his patient descent into these lower depths, the conviction grows that normal, civilized man is actually a combination of child, savage, and madman. If he is in fact these things, what sort of City can he hope to build? Freud examines that City in *Civilization and Its Discontents*.

Has human life any purpose? "One can hardly go

wrong," answers Freud, "in concluding that the idea
of a purpose in life stands and falls with the religious
system." And Freud cannot accept a religious system. "We will turn, therefore, to the less ambitious
problem: what the behaviour of men themselves re-
veals as the purpose and object of their lives, what
they demand of life and wish to attain in it. The
answer to this can hardly be in doubt: they seek happiness, they want to become happy and to remain
so. . . . As we see, it is simply the pleasure-princi-
ple which draws up the programme of life's purpose." [125] As for religion, "The religions of humanity, too, must be classified as mass-delusions. . . ." [126]

But man's goal of happiness is threatened from
three sources: "the three sources of human sufferings, namely, the superior force of nature, the disposition to decay of our bodies, and the inadequacy of
our methods of regulating human relations in the
family, the community, and the state." [127] There is
in us, indeed, a definite "hostility to civilization";
and Freud speculates that this may derive in part
from the Christian tradition, which from its formation denounced the pagan culture around it, and in
part from our voyages in recent centuries among
primitive peoples, who seemed to us—incorrectly,
thinks Freud—to be freer and happier than ourselves. The reader will have no difficulty in recall-
ing how clearly Rousseau manifested this "hostility
to civilization."

Man has tamed and used nature until he "has
nearly become a god himself," [128] but he demands
more from civilization than this control over his
physical environment. He demands beauty, cleanli-

ness, order. He demands "intellectual, scientific, and aesthetic achievement" [129]—in short, "ideas." Finally, men unite in civilization to make law. "The strength of this united body is then opposed as *right* against the strength of any individual, which is condemned as *brute force*." [130] What that united body desires is then considered "justice." But Freud can see no higher justice in the force of the group than in the force of an individual. And he asks himself one of Rousseau's questions: How did civilization, or "culture," which enslaves us all, come about?

Freud is convinced it came about as the result of the deepest urge or impulse or drive in man: the sexual urge. This urge, which he baldly calls "genital love," has been "sublimated" into friendship— the friendship that Aristotle and Montesquieu and Rousseau alike recognized as the necessary basis for community and even government. The original aim of this sexual drive was "inhibited," re-directed, and now furnishes the social adhesiveness of every human community. But love, having created the community, and ultimately the state, necessarily clashes with it. The family group clashes with the larger community. Woman's desire for personal love clashes with man's work, into which the community has found means of forcing him to sublimate his sexual urge. Indeed, civilization drains from its members the very energies that would, without civilization, express themselves in sexual love. It is precisely the community's determination to drain these energies that constantly create taboos, even in primitive societies. Finally, civilization will say to us: "Thou shalt love thy neighbor as thyself" and even

"Love thine enemies." For we not only love; we are aggressive. And civilization finds it necessary to bind us together with such commands—commands, incidentally, which Freud holds we cannot possibly fulfill. The Communists, of course, will tell us that it is private property and exploitation that make men aggressive. But Freud will not believe it. He is certain that these deep instincts of aggression, which we constantly disclose in our early childhood and in our later dream-life, antedate any system of property. In fact, this aggressiveness is one of our chief reasons for living in communities: "There is an advantage, not to be undervalued, in the existence of smaller communities, through which the aggressive instinct can find an outlet in enmity towards those outside the group. It is always possible to unite considerable numbers of men, in love towards one another, so long as there are still some remaining as objects of aggressive manifestations." [131] Jews, suggests Freud—himself a Jew—serve the German imperialist in this way, as the bourgeois serves the Russian communist.

Freud holds that the conscious part of our minds, the "ego," determines us to self-preservation; but our libido-instincts drive us to love others, though sometimes, as in sadism, perversely and cruelly. When the ego and the libido clash; then, even if the ego emerges victorious, it pays the price of victory in a "neurosis." This mental disorder expresses itself in various complex symptoms. Moreover, along with our love-instincts, our libido, we human beings apparently have a deep destruction-instinct, a death-instinct. Thus Eros and Death both drive us, but in different directions: "And now, it seems to me, the meaning of the evolution of culture is no longer a riddle to us. It must present to us the struggle between Eros and Death, between the instincts of life and the instincts of destruction, as it works itself out in the human species. This struggle is what all life essentially consists of and so the evolution of civilization may be simply described as the struggle of the human species for existence. And it is this battle of the Titans that our nurses and governesses try to compose with their lullaby-song of Heaven!" [132]

In order to protect itself against the aggressive instincts of the individual, civilization arouses in us a sense of guilt. But, retorts Freud, this "conscience" is merely an aggression against our ego. It appears in childhood as the *"dread of losing love"*—[133] which in turn involves loss of protection and hence threatens the instinct of self-preservation—or it even appears as a dread of direct punishment by others. It is "internalized" in us as a "super-ego." It is the super-ego that gives us a "bad conscience" when we are doing certain things which we are nevertheless driven by our innermost impulses to do. This command of the cultural super-ego presents itself in its most august aspect as the idea of God, an idea ultimately reducible to a father-image.

Freud is only too aware of the necessities which lead civilization to develop these restraints of conscience, this super-ego, in its members. But as this super-ego steps up its power to keep pace with the growing complexities of civilization, its conflict with the rebelling ego is so severe that Freud sympathizes with those who say of civilization, its aims, and its means that "one is bound to conclude that the whole thing is not worth the effort and that in the end it can only produce a state of things which no individual will be able to bear." [134] Before the reader condemns Freud for harboring this sympathy with anarchy, he would do well to study him carefully; for the internal conflicts that Freud has studied and recorded, together with their social prevalence, give one pause.

Freud therefore cannot share Marx's cheerful view of the future, once the classless society of workers has been set up. On all sides he sees signs of mounting psychic tension, a tension which he would not expect Communism to abolish, a tension between "the death instinct" and Eros. "Men have brought their powers of subduing the forces of nature to such a pitch that by using them they could now very easily exterminate one another to the last man. They know this—hence arises a great part of their current unrest, their dejection, their mood of apprehension. And now it may be expected that the other of the two *heavenly forces,* eternal Eros, will put forth his strength so as to maintain himself alongside of his equally immortal adversary." [135] Why one may now expect this, Freud does not clearly say. Perhaps if Freudian man can manage to sublimate enough of his sexual urge into the super-ego, he can bear the state of things which civilization imposes, without going mad in the process.

Men have ascribed to the wisdom of Solon the advice: "Know thyself." It was Socrates who declared that the unexamined life is not worth living. The

Christian tradition taught the duty of self-examination; and the Christian Church instituted to that end the practice of confession. Freudian psychoanalysis, too, is a kind of Socratic device for leading the patient to know himself, his motives, his passions. But it is significant that whereas Greek philosopher and Christian theologian alike pictured man's mind as "acting" when it thinks and as "suffering" or "passive" when it experiences "passions," Freud sees in passion an active force, of which thoughts are a sort of derivative. Freudian man is not so much driven by passion; he is himself passion-energy. At least that is what his unconscious is, and his unconscious plays a far more dominant role than does his conscious mind. In short, man is more like the irrational animals than he has usually liked to suppose. He is certainly nearer infantilism, nearer madness, nearer savagery, and nearer poetry than he generally suspects. When he appears adult, sane, civilized, and literal, you have but to read his dreams to find what wild longings possess him, what dreadful deeds he would perform, how torn he is between Eros and Destruction, how great the drama in the human heart.

The conversation is ended. A list of books confronts us, books in which men of extraordinary genius, but with varying and often contrary views of what human life means, argue with each other about those views or create poetic symbols of them to persuade us of their truth. The books I selected out to deal with in this essay are those which argued about what is to be done, what aims are worth choosing, by what means those purposes may be attained. All these books were written with faith, even those that appear most skeptical; all of them were written at least in the faith that they could be understood. To be read well, they must be read with the same faith. A few of them are genuinely difficult, and they tempt the average reader to turn elsewhere in order that some book that is easier to read will tell him what is in these books. But there are no other books that tell what is in these books better than these books tell, or even as well as they do. Some of them cost many years of loving labor to write; they are certainly worth hours of loving labor, of reading and rereading, if one would understand them. Some were written a far time from now and in a far place from here; but they are always a time and place worth visiting for those who want to understand. If the reader wants to discuss them with others who live here and now, he will be wise to do it after reading them, not before. The ideas that they contain are the private property of no man: they belong to every man who grasps them.

Myriads of human beings have had the exciting experience of trying to read books in some tongue they do not know, or to speak such a tongue; and have discovered that words, whether written or spoken, are inherently intelligible for those who have the faith to keep on reading or to keep on listening. This faith every two-year-old seems to possess, although he often loses it by the time he is ten or twelve. Some of the books I have discussed here seem frighteningly obscure to those who do not know them, until one fine day the person willing to

read them and re-read them finds them unbeliev-
ably more luminous than most books he has read.

Collections of books like these offer the reader
enduring friendships with some of the most spacious
and exciting minds that we have any record of.
Those readers who have made the patient effort to
enter such minds can never again know the loneli-
ness that many of their neighbors undergo. For although billions of voices have spoken, the books on
the list here discussed are among the voices that
endured.

In this essay I have said little either about poems,
dramas, and novels or about books that bear on
mathematics and the nature of matter. I have spoken
almost exclusively of books that try to say what a
good human life is and what a good human community is like. These books ask many questions,
and try to answer them. In every case, perhaps, the
answers will repel some reader; but if he will give
them the hospitality of his mind, he may live to be
thankful that he never turned an idea from his door,
even a hateful one. For hateful guests can be ex-
traordinarily informative. Some of the answers, on
the other hand, the reader may feel he already
knows, either by proof or by faith. If by proof, he
may find his proof interestingly challenged. If by
faith, should he not know more completely through
the dialectic of these books what it is that by faith
he holds?

Let us, then, take counsel of the great, not in order either to agree or disagree with what they say,
but to understand it and ponder it. In any case, if
we read listeningly the writers discussed in this essay,

we cannot find them boring. For that, their subject is our sure guarantee. For if you were now to ask me, What are these books about? I should without hesitation answer: These books, my reader, were written about you.

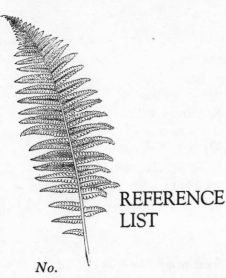

REFERENCE LIST

No.

1. The Complete Works of Homer, *The Odyssey,* trans. by S. H. Butcher and A. Lang (New York, Modern Library, 1950) page 188.

2. Homer, *The Iliad,* I, viii, trans. by A. T. Murray, The Loeb Classical Library (London, W. Heinemann, 1928) page 361.

3. Thucydides, *History of the Peloponnesian War,* trans. by Richard Crawley, Everyman's Library (London, J. M. Dent, 1910) page 15.

4. Plato's *Dialogues, Meno,* trans. by B. Jowett (New York, Random House, 1937) page 366.

5. *Ibid.,* page 378.

6. Plato's *Dialogues, Apology,* trans. by B. Jowett (New York, Random House, 1937) page 406.

7. Plato's *Dialogues, The Republic,* I, trans. by B. Jowett (New York, Random House, 1937) page 851.

8. *The Stoic and Epicurean Philosophers—Meditations,* iv, trans. by G. Long (New York, Modern Library, 1957) page 509.

No.

9. *The Stoic and Epicurean Philosophers—Manual,* trans. by P. E. Matheson (New York, Modern Library, 1957) page 483.

10. *The Confessions of St. Augustine,* trans. by E. D. Pusey, Everyman's Library, 1950, 1966, page 163.

11. *Ibid.,* page 194.

12. *Ibid.,* page 195.

13. St. Augustine, *Treatise on The City of God,* xi, trans. by F. R. Montgomery Hitchcock (London, Society for Promoting Christian Knowledge, 1931) page 188.

14. Latin Works of Dante Alighieri, *Letter to Can Grande,* trans. by A. G. C. Howell and Philip H. Wicksteed, The Temple Classics (London, J. M. Dent, 1904) page 351.

15. Thomas Hobbes, *Leviathan,* reprinted from the Edition of 1651 (Oxford, Clarendon Press, 1929) pages 284–5.

16. *Ibid.,* page 75.

17. *Ibid.,* page 48.

18. *Ibid.,* page 44.

19. *Ibid.,* page 160.

20. *Ibid.,* page 544.

21. *Ibid.,* pages 96–7.

22. *Ibid.,* page 98.

23. *Ibid.,* page 131.

24. *Ibid.,* page 132.

No.

25. William Shakespeare, *Hamlet,* Act II, Scene ii, Lines 310–320 (London, J. M. Dent & Co., 1908) page 61.

26. Benedictus de Spinoza, *Ethics,* trans. by A. Boyle, Everyman's Library (New York, E. P. Dutton, 1959) page 192.

27. *Ibid.,* pages 223–4.

28. *Ibid.,* page 224.

29. Hobbes, *Leviathan,* page 97.

30. John Locke, *Two Treatises on Civil Government,* Everyman's Library (London, J. M. Dent, 1959) page 119.

31. *Ibid.,* page 118.

32. *Ibid.,* page 241.

33. Hobbes, *Leviathan,* page 189.

34. Locke, *Of Civil Government,* page 130.

35. *Ibid.,* page 130.

36. *Ibid.,* page 180.

37. *Ibid.,* pages 139–40.

38. *Ibid.,* page 191.

39. Hobbes, *Leviathan,* page 98.

40. John Locke, *A Letter Concerning Toleration* (New York, D. Appleton Century, 1937) page 186.

41. *Ibid.,* page 212.

42. John Milton, *Areopagitica,* Everyman's Library (London, J. M. Dent, 1946) page 15.

No.

43. *Ibid.,* page 37.

44. Locke, *A Letter Concerning Toleration,* page 205.

45. Jean Jacques Rousseau, "A Discourse on Political Economy," *The Social Contract and Discourses,* trans. by G. D. H. Cole, Everyman's Library (New York, E. P. Dutton, 1950) page 254.

46. Rousseau, *The Social Contract and Discourses,* page 14.

47. *Ibid.,* page 15.

48. Rousseau, *The Social Contract,* page 22 note.

49. *Ibid.,* page 33.

50. *Ibid.,* page 117.

51. *Ibid.,* page 121.

52. *Ibid.,* page 85.

53. *Ibid.,* page 85 note.

54. Rousseau, "The Origin of Inequality," *The Social Contract and Discourses,* page 207.

55. Rousseau, "A Discourse on Political Economy," *The Social Contract and Discourses,* page 256.

56. Edward Gibbon, *The Decline and Fall of the Roman Empire* (New York, Modern Library, 1960) I, page 1.

57. *Ibid.,* page 153.

58. Immanuel Kant, *Metaphysics of Ethics,* trans. by Otto Manthey-Zorn (New York, D. Appleton Century, 1938) page 38.

No.

59. Rousseau, "A Discourse on Political Economy," *The Social Contract and Discourses,* page 254.

60. Locke, *Of Civil Government,* page 191.

61. Rousseau, *The Social Contract,* page 85 note.

62. Charles de Secondat Montesquieu, *The Spirit of Laws,* trans. by Thomas Nugent, Hafner Library of Classics (New York, Hafner, 1949) Vol. I, page 127.

63. *Ibid.,* page 126.

64. United States Constitution, Preamble.

65. Adam Smith, *The Wealth of Nations,* Everyman's Library (London, J. M. Dent, 1933–4) Vol. I, page 12.

66. *Ibid.,* page 389.

67. *Ibid.,* page 400.

68. *Ibid.,* page 15.

69. *Ibid.,* page 8.

70. Hobbes, *Leviathan,* page 97.

71. Smith, *The Wealth of Nations,* Vol. I, page 13.

72. *Ibid.,* p. 26.

73. *Ibid.,* page 28.

74. *Ibid.,* page 57.

75. *Ibid.,* page 58.

76. *Ibid.,* pages 58–9.

77. *Ibid.,* page 59.

78. *Ibid.,* page 117.

79. *Ibid.,* pages 230, 232.

No.

80. *Ibid.,* page 249.

81. *Ibid.,* page 256.

82. *Ibid.,* page 397.

83. *Ibid.,* page 408.

84. *Ibid.,* Vol. II, page 154.

85. *Ibid.,* page 156.

86. *Ibid.,* Vol. I, page 436.

87. *Ibid.,* page 400.

88. J. S. Mill, *Utilitarianism, Liberty, Representative Government,* Everyman's Library (New York, E. P. Dutton, 1951) page 6.

89. *Ibid.,* page 9.

90. *Ibid.,* page 14.

91. *Ibid.,* page 49.

92. *Ibid.,* page 51.

93. *Ibid.,* pages 72–3.

94. *Ibid.,* page 75.

95. *Ibid.,* page 81.

96. *Ibid.,* page 84.

97. *Ibid.,* page 94.

98. *Ibid.,* page 95.

99. *Ibid.,* page 96.

100. *Ibid.,* page 97.

101. *Ibid.,* page 103.

102. *Ibid.,* page 104.

103. *Ibid.,* page 104.

No.

104. *Ibid.,* page 104.

105. *Ibid.,* pages 124–5.

106. *Ibid.,* page 170.

107. *Ibid.,* page 280.

108. *Ibid.,* page 308 note.

109. *Ibid.,* page 310.

110. *Ibid.,* page 299.

111. *Ibid.,* pages 368–9, 373.

112. Rousseau, *The Social Contract,* page 22 note.

113. Karl Marx, *Capital,* trans. by Samuel Moore and Edward Aveling, Great Books of the Western World (Chicago, Encyclopaedia Britannica Inc., 1952) Ch. I, page 20.

114. *Ibid.,* page 21 note.

115. *Ibid.,* Ch. VI, pages 83–4.

116. *Ibid.,* Ch. XIV, page 173.

117. *Ibid.,* page 176.

118. *Ibid.,* Ch. XV, page 180.

119. *Ibid.,* pages 180–1.

120. *Ibid.,* Ch. XXXI, page 377 note 3.

121. *Ibid.,* Ch. XXXIII, pages 381–2.

122. *Ibid.,* page 380.

123. Karl Marx, *The Communist Manifesto,* trans. by Samuel Moore and Edward Aveling, Great Books of the Western World (Chicago, Encyclopaedia Britannica Inc., 1952) Ch. I, pages 424–5.

124. *Ibid.,* Ch. IV, page 434.

No.

125. Sigmund Freud, *Civilization and Its Discontents,* original trans. by Joan Riviere, Great Books of the Western World (Chicago, Encyclopaedia Britannica Inc., 1952) page 772. Reprinted from *Civilization and Its Discontents,* Translated from the German and Edited by James Strachey. By permission of W. W. Norton & Company, Inc., New York, N.Y. Copyright © 1961 by James Strachey.

126. *Ibid.,* page 774.

127. *Ibid.,* page 776.

128. *Ibid.,* page 778.

129. *Ibid.,* page 780.

130. *Ibid.,* page 780.

131. *Ibid.,* page 788.

132. *Ibid.,* page 791.

133. *Ibid.,* page 792.

134. *Ibid.,* page 801.

135. *Ibid.,* page 802.